SET THE TONE

The Speaker & Coach's Guide to Generating Massive Revenue Using Professional Audio/Visual Production

by Darrin Thompson

www.cleftonegrooves.com

PUBLISHER
Clef Tone Grooves

Bloomington, IL

December 2017

Table of Contents

<u>Foreword by Dr. Ruben West</u>

Albert Einstein said you can't solve a problem with the same level of thinking that it took to create the problem. And for so many speakers and coaches and trainers who do live broadcast, the problem is they're not making the money that they want to make. What I love about Darrin Thompson is he's come up with a way to figure out how to crack to code and solve that money problem.

Imagine a diamond in a jewelry store that was just sitting in a box it wasn't well lit, it wasn't well displayed. What they know is they will never command top dollar for that diamond! So what they do is they put the right lighting on it, and they put it in the exact display case, and they have it wrapped in a black cloth so that it hides the background color and really illuminates the colors within the diamond. What Darrin does, is he shows us how to do the exact same thing with our message.

How do we choose the right microphone? How do we choose the right lighting? How do we choose the right background set so that when we give our message, it shines like a diamond?

This book is going to help you discover the new level of thinking that it takes to solve the money problem.

QUALITY
COMMANDS
PAYMENT!

That goes for diamonds, and that also goes for *your* message!

Endorsement:

To establish yourself as an expert in the market place you must be able to deliver. Not just deliver but truly be able to deliver at the highest level! Being a coach, speaker, or both, the way in which we communicate is imperative to make an impact. Often times because of our passion for what we're doing, we focus greatly on the message and content. Once the message is crafted and we're extremely confident of it's potential to impact, we forget one of the most critical pieces…

We forget the "how" it will be heard! One of the best ways to ensure you're able to optimize your message's reach and delivery, is quality audio!

Within the following work Darrin over delivers on the crucial steps you can take to separate yourself in the market place as you begin to position yourself within your given niche as an authority.

A lot of times we can underestimate the overall quality of our works, not realizing this could very well have a lot to do with "how" our message is received by our audience. There is a wealth of information that Darrin provides for you to really be able to hit the ground running right out of the box ensuring your sound is in line with the strength of your message.

Having an opportunity to work with Darrin & Clef Tone Grooves directly, he truly knows his stuff and is very passionate about his craft. When it comes to the quality audio and sound of my message, Clef Tone Grooves is indeed my go to!

While you focus on providing life changing information and "dropping the mic" don't hesitate to apply what's on the pages within and Darrin's expertise to ensure you really "Don't Drop The Mic"!

Darrin goes above and beyond in this piece just as he does in going the extra mile for his clients. I'm confident he can provide you with the same professional quality I've been able to add to my audio/visual digital products and more.

Let's BUILD!

Cori G. Briggs
Creator of The Builder's
Workshop
Speaker | Author | Coach

www.thebuildersworkshop.com

<u>Preface</u>

I'd like to personally thank you for investing your time in learning how to capture your audio/visual content in a professional way…but I can't because I'm not there in person. So this next sentence is for you…

Where ever you may be, *whoever* you may be — THANK YOU!

By investing in this publication, you've invested in yourself, and investing in yourself is ALWAYS a good thing. It really means a lot to me that you're taking time to learn just some of the basics behind producing better media for those whose lives you hope to change along the way.

So one more time, THANK YOU!

In an audio/visual production environment, one of the things audio engineers do is send a signal out to cameras and other devices to make sure that signal is being received on the other end. This is called sending "tone". Do a search on youtube for a 1 kilohertz sine wave sound, and you'll hear that familiar sound I'm referring to. In addition to making sure the signal is being received, when audio engineers send tone, it's a consistent audio source they can use to set levels on the devices receiving the sound. So you could say, that audio engineers "set the tone". And much like audio engineers, when you, the motivational coach, host a conference, you too "set the tone". When you create audio/visual content for your websites, and social media — you "set the tone".

For all the public speakers who are just getting started, building their brands — ultimately their careers, and who are learning to harness the power of audio/visual technology — I wrote this book to help you *set the tone*. I want to help you *set the tone* for how others perceive your brand, and by doing so, increase your exposure, expand your influence, and grow your revenue. What person, in business for themselves today, doesn't want that?

But, with so many people playing in the digital space these days, how does one stand out?

In a word: **quality**.

In actions: **deliberate**.

With your media: **well produced — Tone setting! Know your purpose.**

I am a strong believer that in today's competitive environment, you have to actively start thinking of the quality of your audio/visual content as part of your brand. I say "actively" because far too many people treat their content quality as an afterthought. When people overlook the importance of audio/visual quality in their branding they're overlooking the impression they're leaving on their audience. If you commit this sin in this digital age, you've overlooked your brand. Your tone is out of whack!

Now some people may be savvy enough to know that they need to look good on video and have decent lighting, and maybe even a nice camera to boot. But even in that camp, while folks concern themselves with how good they look on camera, audio quality is almost *never* considered, if it's even considered at all. Don't get me wrong, I like to look good on camera too! HD for the win "all day, erry day!" But while you're lining up your pretty shots, I want you to think about this for a second…

…Well…for much longer than a second…Anyways…

Aside from your mind — as a motivational speaker and coach, what are the two main tools you use the most? Most likely you'd say, your *voice* (<u>audio</u>), and your *message* (usually conveyed <u>audibly</u>).

Then think about these next questions:

How can you motivate or influence others to act if the quality of your audio is lacking?

How many of those people will click off to another video because of lackluster production quality — audio *and* video?

How many of those people watching your videos are being introduced to your brand for the first time?

Using lackluster production, how many of those first-timers will take your brand, your message, and ultimately *you* seriously?

Bottom line — How many of those people do you expect to convert into paying clientele?

Bonus Question: Would *you* buy from someone whose media quality was lackluster?

And as you think about those questions I also want you to think about what matters to you most. Why do you shoot your videos? Why do you share your voice and your message? It's not only because you want to be *seen*, but most importantly because you want to be…(*I know you already finished my sentence*).

Listen, You have a message worth sharing! You have a brand worth expanding! You cannot afford to cheat either one because you have revenue that needs growing!

I know how frustrating it is when you have a message you're passionate about, but yet no one else seems to want to listen…so why provide any additional reasons for your message not to be heard?

Now, not every piece of media you share needs to be a slickly produced, highly polished masterpiece, but on the flip-side not every piece of media you produce needs to be done with the camera and microphone on your cell phone either! However, I'd hope that you'd take a little pride in your productions *more often* than not.

I'm not saying that just because your A/V quality dramatically increases that you'll start getting paid opportunities everywhere and life will be grand, but *anyone* who wants to be taken seriously needs to first start taking themselves and their brand seriously — A/V quality included.

The will to prepare is the will to succeed.

While you read this book, what's shared herein may seem like a lot of obvious, insignificant steps to take for some of you. Just keep in mind that when you put all these tips and tools to use "in concert," it will add up to big results in the end. When it comes to production, there is no *one* tool, no *one* trick, no *one-giant-leap* that will serve as a "magic bullet" to making your productions professional grade. Rather it's a myriad of small *deliberate* steps that add up as a whole overall.

The small deliberate actions I outline in this publication are things you can do to set yourself apart when it comes to producing content in the digital space.

If you read and apply even just *some* of the tips I share in this publication, I promise you *will* get better results on your future productions!

While I won't say there's a right way and a wrong way to capture audio and video, I will say that there's "one way," and then there's "a better way…always." I'd like to temper that thought with another…That *how* you capture audio and video can be highly subjective. There are many ways to achieve the same outstanding results. As the captain of your ship, manager of your brand, "Setter of the tone", it will be up to you to decide how you want to reach that "professional" destination. So please keep in mind that this isn't an end-all-be-all, authoritative publication on the "only way" to capture audio and video in a professional manner. This is simply *one* way to capture it in a professional manner…my way, a way that has served me well, time and again for over 15 years even with subpar equipment. And now I'm sharing my way with you.

I've taken the time to provide you with an index at the end of the book, as well as one online. The index at the end of the book provides very useful documents and tips on using them. The online index is where you'll find my recommendations on gear and tips for using it. I highly advise you to just read through the book once, and worry about the gear afterwards. You can have all the top-of-line gear in the world but still capture crappy audio and crappy video! Once you've captured crappy media, it's hard to make it look and sound good after the fact…

Yeah…it's hard to polish a turd…jus' sayin'…

So learn to drive this "car" called audio/visual before you go out and wreck your "Ferrari".

Some of the knowledge I share in this book can get specific to certain types of gear like microphones and other accessories, but when I just talk about things like audio or lighting in general, those tips can be applied pretty much across the board whether you have pro gear, or gear you wish was pro.

Please remember as you're reading away in this book, working to improve the quality of your media, why you picked up this book in the first place. Production isn't your ultimate focus, only a means to an end. A means to help put you, your message, and your brand's best foot forward. To quickly get the best results out of your gear, my recommendation to you, the reader, would be to simply try the methods I present here first, and then adjust them to your needs once you've got the concepts down.

With that said, if you're ready to up your game and be a Tone Setter, then keep reading!

1. <u>Act Like a Director, Think Like an Audio Engineer</u>

For the last decade I've had the privilege to be involved with countless audio/visual productions from a corporate, brand-managed perspective, and more recently through gaining tons of projects of my own.

I've recorded in high-end audio booths with microphones that would make any audiophile drool, worked with cameras and lighting that were woefully worth more than my annual salary, and have even done makeup for professional talent before going on set…Heck! I've even done my own makeup before going on camera. Yes, I know what you're thinking…For the record, yes, I have worn makeup…on numerous occasions. More to come on that later.

There's so much more to share about my years of experience, but for now, I say all of what I just said to say, *"Yeah…I have a pretty good idea of what I'm doing."* So on to the reason you picked up this book in the first place.

Before we go any further, I need you to *Act like a director, think like an audio engineer.*

Huh?!

If I could see your face right now, I'm sure it has an interesting look on it, but that's exactly what I mean.

Let's face it, if you're someone who is technologically challenged, if the only pictures or videos you've ever taken were of your cat coughing up hairballs that looked like Michael Jackson *(or so you thought)*, or you've just plain never shot a professional video before, then there's a strong chance that you're not acting like a director, or thinking like an audio engineer. And why should you be that way?! It's not like it's your day job. Only crazy people take on roles that cause them to think this way!

…Oh wait…I digress.

Let's be clear, this is through no fault of your own. You simply don't know what you don't know and there's nothing wrong with that…until you know.

So what exactly do I mean when I say "Act like a director, think like an Audio Engineer?"

Well, I'm trying to introduce a new mindset, a new pattern of thinking through how you execute on your productions, a very particular mindset or pattern that will cause you to be aware of *what* you're doing on that production and why.

Think about what directors do on set…and no, they don't just call, "Action!" They do way more than that. But for the sake of you acting like them, some key takeaways are that they visualize how they want the scene to look, and from what angles they want to capture that scene. They think about things like camera movements *(if there are any)* and how they want lighting to look, physically putting their eyes into the angles they want the cameras to be at, and maybe even mimicking the camera movements themselves to get an idea of how it will look when they get the camera in place, and then some. They'll also think about where they want everything to be that will be visible in the final shot.

Audio Engineers "think with their ears." They listen to the environment around them, taking into account any running HVAC systems, appliances, foot and motor traffic. They get an estimation of the battles they'll have to fight in order to capture the cleanest audio possible and they often look for ways to control the environment around them as much as possible to ensure they only capture the sounds they want to hear. They also think about things like where to hide microphones if they are required to be out of the shot.

There's so much more to it than that, and there are many more roles I could add into the mix like writers, producers, set designers, production assistants, and more, but what I want you to take away from this chapter is that when you're creating media, you need to have what I call a "production mindset".

(#productionmindset - After reading this book, share your pics, videos, and other posts on Facebook and Instagram using this hashtag to show how you took your media quality to the next level!)

You probably won't be the next Steven Spielberg, nor will you likely be capturing sound on the set of the latest Marvel Superhero movie, but if I can just get you to understand that production is more than simply setting up a camera in "any-ol'-room" and using the built-in microphone on said camera to pick up your voice or other sounds, then I will have gotten through to you…maybe.

Yes, having a production mindset means you will *deliberately plan out* your production before you go to execute. Now, this doesn't have to be some elaborate plan with storyboarding and all that, but gathering as much detail as you can think of going into a project, significantly affects the end results coming out as well as how smooth you work through that project. That may also involve thinking of things like whether or not you should use a script.

Another aspect of having a production mindset includes holding yourself to a higher standard of performance quality, especially if the video is *recorded* vs. *live*. Some of you being public speakers, performance is something you most likely won't have a problem with. However, if you have an awkward pause during a take, or you miss a word, go back. Shoot it until you get it right, until you get it the way you want it. If you sway back and forth, or perform any other distracting action in your video while you're recording, go back…Re-shoot it and for gosh sake stop swaying! Of course unless, it's on purpose…could be interesting I guess…

If you have a production mindset, it means you're hyper-aware of your set, how you look on camera, how you sound, how the set looks, how your recording environment sounds, how you deliver your message, how it gets edited in post…All of it. It means taking an active role in your production from beginning to end and not settling for "doing it the way you've always done it," or following the path of least resistance, but realizing you owe it to your brand and your future clients not to settle for anything less than professional. So…how bad is your "good enough"?

2. <u>Act II…Hold The Butter</u>

Now that we've got you in the right mindset and you're more aware of *how* you'll execute your production, it's time to think about crafting your message for your next production.

For example, if your overarching message is something like empowerment, or personal finance, what key points about your message do you want to share in your next video?

Keep in mind who your audience will be as well. This can also help you to set some parameters on your next video, such as how long you think the video should be, how much information to share, what to share in the next video after this one, etc…

Let's use the example of personal finance…Maybe the message in your next video is going to be on budgeting and why that's so important if you want financial freedom.

Think about the key aspects in that message (*Keep in mind these are really rough examples, and by no means am I a "financial genius"*):

Example

Why should you have a budget?

- It helps you be disciplined in your spending habits
- It helps you keep track of your expenses

What are the benefits of having a budget?

- *By keeping track of your expenses you know what shape your finances are in*

- *Rather than restricting you, a budget empowers you to make educated decisions on how to move forward to a state of financial freedom*

Do you see what's starting to form here? An outline! Now, all you need is an open and close for this topic.

Might I recommend in your close, that you whet your audience's appetite by dropping a hint as to what next week's topic will cover? So today you talked about why people should have a budget, and the benefits of it. In your close, maybe you ask them to come back to see exactly how to do a budget in the next video! And it goes without saying to follow up with the next video doing exactly that. If you don't, make sure you have a sensible reason why you didn't keep your promise, but still at least acknowledge what you said previously.

Now, back to your outline…

Once you add an open and close, the cool part is that you *could* use this as the building blocks to your script, if you decide to use one, or at the very least keep it as is and use those bullet points to jog your memory while on camera and speak extemporaneously.

A few side notes on scripts and outlines:

Many a great public speaker knows this information but for those who don't — first and foremost if you use any notes at all while delivering your message, I'll always recommend using the outline with just a few bullet points over a fully fleshed out, word-for-word script. Using outlines with simple bullet points frees you up to be able to speak more sincerely, and give life to your delivery. It keeps you on message just about as good as a full-blown script. If you can go over your outline and keep it well in mind during your delivery, this method by far is the gold standard in my book.

If you choose to read a script word for word, know that it *can* be done…Newscasters do it all the time, and make it sound like they are speaking directly to you. That's the key though, they *make it sound like they are speaking directly to you.* A lot of times though, they are reading from a teleprompter.

Reading from a script is nice, because you have all your words in front of you. However, this method also takes more time. More time to type it all out, more time to rehearse it, and usually more time to deliver it and get that perfect take.

Keep in mind if you read from a script though, you might have to fight a few problems that feed into each other:

1. Reading a script can cause you to lose focus on your message as you work harder to focus on getting the words right.

2. Because you focus on the words more, your delivery can easily slip into a monotonous, rhythmic reading of your lines, rather than an enthusiastic delivery. *(Your goal is to motivate people to do something…right?)*

3. Because you'll be in the midst of recording take after take to get your lines right, you most likely won't catch your monotonous rhythmic reading until you go to edit your video. By this time, depending on how good you are, you may have spent more time than you wanted on something that turned out not so great.

Once you've got your message crafted, and especially if you've decided to write out a whole script, practice out loud. I would also recommend doing this in front of a mirror so you can see yourself in your full glory…or maybe your "half glory" if your delivery needs work. Sometimes what you write down on paper and hear inside your head comes out sounding totally different even *terrible* when audibly verbalized. So read aloud.

This next topic may or may not apply to you, but I did want to touch on it just a little bit — the teleprompter. All the same thoughts I mentioned earlier on reading from a fully developed script will apply. When reading from a teleprompter, even though you're looking directly at the camera, you can still come across to your audience as if you're just reading…because you are. The only difference is that now your script is on the glass in front of the camera lens. Using a prompter does not necessarily make you deliver your lines better. Delivery still depends on you. "No magic bullet," remember? Even worse, if you *do* get lulled into just reading your script, it can also come across as insincere, like you don't know your own message. So again, the trick is deliver your message in a way that is lively, enthusiastic, and like you're having a nice conversation with your friend who is standing right in front of you. You've got to show the camera some LOVE!

The next thing is just a personal pet peeve of mine — earlier I mentioned that reading from a script can easily get you into a "monotonous, rhythmic" reading. What I mean is, as you get rolling, you may start reading every sentence with the same inflection. You may start and end every sentence the same way, emphasizing the same parts of each sentence with the same tone of voice. Imagine if you met someone for the first time and you spoke to them like that. DON'T DO IT! This is one of the quickest indications to your audience that you *are in fact* reading from a script, and again it sounds disingenuous.

3. <u>Lewis & Clark</u>

With your message now ready for an audience, it's time to go on an expedition…around your house. Scout for a location from which you will share your message with the world.

Some of you may decide to use a location outside of your home. If you go this route, make sure you obtain permission from the owner of the location you wish to use. Depending on the situation, it might even be a good idea to get permission in writing by typing up your own release that covers all the details that keep you clear of legal remedies, lost revenues, and gets you the kind of access you need to your desired location (*See details about this in the index at the end of this book*).

Whatever the space is that you choose to use, be sure that in some ways, it reflects you, your message, or at the very least what you're about. You want your "set" have some "character" on camera. Using bare, flat, walls as a background is usually not the best way to go, unless you're doing this intentionally. It's also not ideal for getting better audio!

In short, flat surfaces are reflective surfaces, and reflective surfaces bounce unwanted sound back into your microphone. That's called reverb, and if you really want it that bad in your video, add it in post-production, minimize it during the shoot by treating your room for sound (*See the "Good Sound Keeping" Checklist in the index at the end of this book*).

Now, back on topic — Your set needs character. This doesn't mean it has to be over the top with elegant or wild designs, but a little embellishment never hurts. If you have a logo or banner, find some place to display it in the background. Even easier, if you have a branded backdrop that you shoot all your videos with, go for it! Also to consider — do you have a room with a few walls that come together at interesting angles? At the very least maybe you could consider using a corner of your room to help breakup the uniformity of your scene a little bit.

Using your living room with your TV turned on to VH1, having loose cables everywhere, and random objects like an old plate of food on the coffee table next to you does not help your message or brand in any way. Again, would you listen to someone who puts videos out like this?! BE DELIBERATE!

So…start thinking about props. (Cliche Alert: I'm using examples here that a lot of people use) Do you want something like a book case in the background (maybe you've written plenty of books and want them on display), or maybe a little plant life to dress things up? Whatever your message is, it should guide your decisions on what types of props, to have in scene.

And just for men — If you're married don't be afraid to unleash your secret weapon on helping you decorate and design your set…your girlfriend/wife. Women have such an amazing eye for detail! So get them off the bench and into the game.

Next thought, will you be sitting or standing? If sitting, will it be at a table? Will it be at a desk? Will you have your computer or tablet with you on that desk? Etc…Etc..

This book would be a thousand pages long if I listed out every possible consideration so I'll stop while I'm ahead of myself. The point is to be deliberate in choosing not only *your* look, but also that of your set.

> **REMINDER:** *The above considerations are all to help reinforce your production mindset, and that the more details you can decide on now in pre-production the smoother your workflow will be later during production, and post-production.*

Once you've settled on a location, solidify that decision by getting your camera out and framing up the shot. See what the camera sees and determine if you need to tweak your set or shot a little, or if you're even coming close to what you envisioned in your head. I'm sure I don't need to tell you what to do if the shot isn't working.

> <u>**NOTE:**</u> *If you happen to be one of the many folks out there who use your phone as your camera, hopefully you know by now to turn your phone sideways and shoot videos in landscape mode. That's how people want to watch video nowadays, so shoot it that way. Unless you have a really good reason to shoot video with your phone in portrait position (straight up and down), DON'T! It's super annoying to have to look at a skinny screen!*

Once you get your set how you like it, especially if your set is at home, clean it. Make sure you don't have any disheveled piles of papers in scene, or any other items that don't belong on camera. Thinking back to the personal finance example, if that's your message, you don't want a random stack of CDs or a Playstation controller laying around in the shot. It also doesn't hurt to dust your set off every once and while too. And while I don't recommend having large panes of glass on camera — like on a table, or in a window behind you (because of its reflective properties, both audibly and visually), If you choose to use it, clean any smudges and fingerprints off of it.

Put simply, you don't want anything on camera to distract or take away from you or your message — only to complement it. Notice I didn't say *compli<u>i</u>ment*, as in, "Hey there, nice set!" I said *comple<u>e</u>ment* as in, "accessorizes," "perfects," or "completes" you and your message nicely.

<u>Remote Shooting:</u>

There may come times that you have to shoot a video or do a live broadcast outside of your normal setting. I can't stress enough how important it is to continue to *"think like a director"* here. You have an opportunity to capture the attention of newcomers, and even "reward" those who have faithfully tuned into you from the start. Where ever you happen to be for your remote shoot, take time to look around the location for what you think would make for a visually appealing background. Again keep in mind that while no situation is perfect, even here you want to make sure that the background will complement you and your message, not take away from it or distract your viewers.

You'll also want to pay attention to the lighting in your remote setting. This holds especially true for my black peoples! Again because you are not in a controlled environment, the lighting situation will almost always be less than stellar without bringing in your own lights. And it's not like you have to drag a light kit around with you everywhere you go…sometimes all you want to do is a quick shout-out to your viewers. It's these situations that I'm talking about. Do the best you can to make sure you're not shooting in an environment that's so dark that it's hard for you to be seen. Try to find light from a window or otherwise that you can stand near so that it hits you in as flattering a way as possible. If the only light you can find is from directly over head, don't stand directly under it, as this can cause really deep shadows down the front of your face. Instead, step back just a bit to minimize those shadows. More on lighting in the next chapter.

One last thing to consider when shooting remotely — this has more to do with sound and your audience than anything — if you're location happens to be a large wide open space like a cathedral or a hall where there's a lot of reverb, it's going to be next to impossible to control that kind of environment. So in these cases, I recommend not controlling the environment. Instead, let your audience see the space you're recording in, by making it the background behind you. That way it will make sense why there is so much reverb in your environment. I tend to treat other situations the same way. For instance, I see a lot of people at conferences who shoot videos in front of a "red carpet" wall that is branded for that conference. However, when they shoot their videos, there's a lot of background noise from all the other attendees enjoying themselves and having a good time. Sometimes it wouldn't hurt to *see* some of that excitement going on in the background rather than only seeing a branded wall. So get adventurous! If you really want to see branded graphics in the shot, try finding something smaller than an entire wall and try to to capture some of that excitement going on in the background behind you. That way it makes sense why your viewers are hearing the added noise. Let's not forget that some of the folks viewing your video may also be potential clients! So seeing the excitement in the background could also be just what they need to pull the trigger on hiring you for a speaking gig, or to be their coach!

This approach I'm describing here is kind of like, "If you can see it in the shot, it's 'legal'". Not that shooting the other way is illegal by any means.

Anyways, happy trails, Lewis!

4. ...And God Said, "Let There Be Light"...(Because Audio Was Already Working)

Now that you've got your set looking nice, it's time to light it up!

Full disclosure, I've not been trained professionally in all things lighting, but I *do* know you don't want your set looking like the Bat Cave! *Some* light is better than *no* light! Truth be told, I work with lights and learn different ways to use them on a regular basis. The next best thing outside of formal training I'd say. So I'm not a doctor, but I do a little more than just "play one on TV" so-to-speak.

Lighting is much like audio in that you can devote many years to learning this craft and yet still not know all there is to know, and when you think you've found the best way to do something, someone else always has a better way you'll wish you thought of years ago. Plus, new technologies afford us tons of new opportunities to explore this subject all the time. If you want to do additional reading beyond this on lighting, great! For the purposes of this book though, I'll keep it to what you need in order to get started.

Just a quick note if you're shooting your video and doing everything by yourself — Now that you actually need to be in the shot to see how everything looks, it's gonna be super hard to see how everything looks on camera, because you're in front of the camera. A couple of ways you could handle this is to rig up a little handheld mirror from behind your camera so you can see the screen while standing in front of the camera, or if you're not feeling your "inner MacGyver," you can simply record a little footage of you standing in scene and speaking as if you were actually shooting your video for a few seconds and then play it back to make your decisions after the fact.

Nowadays more cameras are also being made with screens that can be faced forward to avoid everything I just said in the last paragraph. Having a camera that does this, I can tell you it has saved me so much time ever since I switched from shooting videos on my cell phone.

This also happens to be a really good time to check head room. Head room is the space in the shot between the top of your head and top of the frame of what the camera sees. A good amount of head room also adds a nice touch to your production quality. All too often, you see people shooting videos with the tops of their heads cut out of the shot, or they have the camera pointed so high that all you see is their head and the ceiling fan spinning above them. TACKY! Head room — not too much, not too…well…none. And yes there are times where cutting off the tops of heads is an okay thing in a video for more artistic purposes, but for straight informational or motivational videos where you're speaking directly to camera and not trying to be artistic, it just looks unprofessional. Again, think about what you are doing, #productionmindset.

Back to lighting!

If you use any kind of professional lighting for your videos, one simple tool you can pick up is a ring light. These are inexpensive and very easy to use.

Another tried and true method is to have three-point lighting. Three-point lighting is where you have one light as your key light, one as your fill light, and a third as a back light to light the set where your shadow is cast from the front two lights. Even without pro lighting the same concept could still be applied with household lamps. It may not look as pretty as professional lighting, but will still help make things a little nicer on camera.

How To Do It:

Set your key light mostly in front of you but a little off to the side to hit you at an angle. *(If you like to angle your body slightly to one side while facing the camera, your key light should be on the side you face).* Set your fill light to your opposite side. For example, if your key is to your left, set your fill to the right. The reason you need a fill light is because if you *only* use a key light you would have shadows on your face where the key light can't get to, like the other side of your nose, and other side of your face. Your fill light "fills" in those shadows by being set up opposite from your key, thus softening or eliminating your shadows.

Lastly, your back light for the set softens or eliminates your shadow that gets cast on the set from your key and fill. *(Key and Peele? NO! Key and fill!)* Setting this light up is as simple as seeing if you've created any shadows of yourself on the set from the positioning of your key and fill lights. Take your position in front of the camera and either look behind you, or use your MacGyver mirror to see where your shadow falls. If you see any shadows that will be in the shot, aim your back light at them.

If you want, you could try adding a fourth light source on yourself to give you a nice edge or rim. You'd place this on the same side as your fill light, but behind you, pointing back at you. This would help further put the focus on you in the shot, and help you "pop" out from your background a little more. Just make sure that this particular light isn't shining into the lens of your camera as it can cause your picture to have a lens flare, and give a washed-out look to your shot. Whatever the height is on your key light, you can match your back light that is aimed at you to that height, or go a bit higher.

If you don't have 3 or 4 lights, use the one or two that you have. You should always have a light that lights you, and if you only have *one* lighting you, bring it a little closer to being in front of you like the camera so that you're lit as good as possible. *(and you know what kind of "lit" I'm talkin' bout!)*

There are some additional things to pay attention to when using any kind of lighting. We've just covered a simple method for positioning your lights in the space *around* you, but properly utilizing the space *above and below* you for positioning is equally important. It can really alter the mood of your video. Remember, you want the light to flatter you on camera. If your lights are in a position where they have to point upward toward you, you could easily wind up looking like you're in a horror film — you know…the flashlight under your chin look with all the scary up-shadows? Queue the lightning strike and creepy organ! Yeah, no…just, no! This can make you look old, and hideous! The only motivating you'll be doing is for people to turn your video off!

If you position your lights too high, you can get long, downward shadows that can be just as distracting. Balance is key. For both vertically and horizontally, you'll want to position your key light in a position where any shadows on your face and neck are minimized. We're talking shadows from your chin over your neck, under your nose, under your eyebrows, places like that. Don't feel bad if you don't get all the shadows! You never will on a small budget. That's why I said "minimize" instead of "get rid of". And again, even at this point, I ask you, what look are you going for with the lighting? Maybe you want shadows to be a certain way. Are you still *acting like a director*?

Positioning your lights also includes how close or far away your lights are from you. The closer the light is on you, the brighter you'll be on camera, but also the more "hot spots" you'll have showing up on your skin on camera and the harsher your shadows will be, and that's not a good thing, especially if you're a person who has oily skin. The farther away the light is, the softer the shadows are, but your features won't be as defined on camera. You may even need to add another light elsewhere on yourself to compensate, or turn up the brightness on your camera, but doing these things can create other headaches for you very quickly. There's a tradeoff. Again, the look you are trying to achieve is key. So how close do you want your lights? A lot of it depends on a combination of, what the light is doing to your features *(mainly your face)*, and if you like it or not.

As for those remaining shadows and hot spots still lingering on your face after meticulously positioning your lights, there are a few methods to address them. There are silks, screens, and anti-shine *(more on anti-shine later)*. Silks are cloths that make the lights softer on the subject being lit, thereby also making the shadows softer as well. They diffuse the light quite a bit. Think about what happens when you take the shade off a lamp when it's on…the whole room gets brighter, you may even find it harder to look in the direction of the lamp. At night time it's even easier to see how harsh the shadows become in the room. A light without a silk can be a lot like that lamp, harsh! A little diffusion is not a bad idea to have on hand.

Screens, knock the hotspots down just a little bit, and diffuse the light to a lesser degree than the silks. There are professionally made screens just for this purpose.

Simply place a silk, or a screen in between you and your light source that's producing the hotspot, and see what affect it has on how you look on camera.

Lights, silks, and screens are all things that can take a bite out of your wallet in a hurry. If you're worried about having professional lighting, listen…It's okay if you don't have professional lighting starting out. Use what you have available to you around the house. The most important thing is to get started. And as an audio guy, I would recommend you focus on getting better sound *first* anyway. Why? Again, you motivate people with your voice, and your message right? You can't shine a light on that…at least not literally, but you *can* turn a really nice mic on and make your message sound oh-so-lovely!

In the meantime, grab a few lamps from around the house that have the flexible necks so you can point and position them how you need to. If you don't have any, you can pick some up just about anywhere these days. As for the expensive silks, frosted white shower curtains make a nice alternative, and for even softer lighting grab other thin materials like white bedsheets to diffuse your light even further. And, if you have no shame, you can achieve great results using the mesh screens right out of your household windows instead of buying the professionally made ones! Double them up for added diffusion! Just keep in mind that using silks, shower curtains, screens, and bed sheets not only soften your shadows, but drops your light levels as well. You may need to compensate for this by moving your lights closer to you, or whatever your subject is that's being lit.

One last thought on lighting yourself, don't wear jewelry that is too blingy on camera. Wearing jewelry is not forbidden, but if it catches the light just right and reflects that into the camera, this can be yet another distraction from your message.

Glasses are another thing to watch out for. If glasses are how people know and see you every day, by all means wear them. Just know that they reflect lights really easily, and that the camera will most likely see lights where your eyes are supposed to be on your face because of that reflection. Anti-glare lenses help knock this down pretty good. You can also try moving your key light further out to your side while still pointing at you, or raising the light a little higher. This doesn't always work, but can help in most cases. If you have lights that are powerful enough, you can try bouncing the light off of a large white surface, like a poster board or foam core, and aim the *bounce* back at you instead of the *light* itself. This can help the light look even more natural and softer on camera whether it's for handling glare in your glasses or just because you like that look, but in order to do this you need a light that has enough power.

Speaking of power, a really handy tool to have for your lighting are dimming switches. This provides a way for you to be able to lower the intensity of the light you're working with so you can dial in your lighting just the way you want it. Just make sure that if you're working with LED or CFL bulbs that they are the kind specified as being dimmable, otherwise when you go to dim the light it will just turn off.

Remember that making all these changes means you'll need to pay attention to what else is being effected in your shot. Are you losing needed light? Is the change causing light to shine on something that you don't want light on? Etc.

Moving on, once you have yourself lit how you like…now you need to consider your set. How do you want the lighting on the set itself to look? Yes, I know you have the back light on the set, but is there anything else special you want to do with lighting? Maybe you want it like the Bat Cave back there behind you, I don't know. But however you light your set, again, it should not take away from you or your message. When you look at your set, and when you look at yourself during playback, your eye shouldn't be drawn to anything but you. You don't want to be lighting up things on your set over abundantly, but in taste, and if you light your set at all, you want it comfortably lit to complement you.

Did you know that color temperature can also make your shot look better on camera? *"What the heck is color temperature?!"* you ask. Take a trip to your local Home Depot or Lowe's and go to the light bulb section. You'll find out very quickly. You'll see lights that say "daylight" (5000 - 6500 Kelvin) and others that say "soft white" (2700 - 3000 Kelvin). This is color temperature. Lights in the 2000-3000K range are more yellow in color and can give your set a "warmer" feel. Tungsten, or 3200K will make it even warmer, adding a hint of orange into your spectrum. 5000K and up emit a blueish white light which gives your set a "cooler" feel.

How this can affect your shot is if you happen to mix color temperatures on your set. Let's say your key light is daylight, but your back light, or other lights on your set are tungsten, it can make your shot look really weird because of the clash of colors.

Think about that feeling you get when you turn on your warm, yellowish overhead lights in your bedroom during a bright, sunny day. Yuck! During the day, that natural daylight appeals to our eye more, so we keep the overhead lights off most of the time.

I want you to try an experiment for me. Surely after reading that last paragraph you've gone to test your overhead lights during the daytime and saw what I was talking about. Now, I want you to get a light bulb that is in the 4500-6000K color temperature range, bring it into your room, and turn it on during the day. Tell me that light doesn't "feel" better and seem to match the natural light coming into your room from the outside.

Paying attention to little details like this bodes well for your videos being more appealing to those who watch them. And when it comes to using a cell phone as your main camera, giving attention to this small detail often helps produce better results. Most cell phone cameras have that auto-focusing/auto white-balancing feature built into them. So having different color temperatures can cause those features to act a little wonky, not knowing which light to focus on as the dominant source. If you ever see the picture dim and come back up to full brightness on your camera, this could be a side effect of poor lighting and mixed color temperatures. This *will* show up in your recording when you go to play it back for review. You don't want that to happen. There are times to mix and match color temperatures, but that's for more complex situations with higher dollar cameras, lights and projects, etc…

So a rule of thumb? Match your color temperatures as best as you can for all your lights. Match them to whatever the dominant source of light is in the location you're shooting in. If you have a ton of daylight coming into your set, or the light you're already using looks blueish-white, go daylight. If you have no daylight coming into scene, you have a little more leeway.

**Note:** Fluorescent overhead lighting tends to be greenish in color on camera. Unless that's the look you want, you may want to turn these off and use different lighting for the room, or look into gels that can correct the color of the light. (See the online index for more info on gels)

If you've purchased special lighting for your videos already, sometimes it's just better to turn off the overhead lighting in the room altogether and just use your special lights by themselves.

If you're really curious what the color temperature is of your lighting, they make color meters for $100 or more. But keeping it simple, especially if you're only using a cell phone to shoot your video, look at the color of the light in your shooting environment. Match accordingly and don't overthink it.

Keep plenty of bulbs handy for the color temperature you need on set. If you have a need to travel with your lights and shoot in multiple locations, having both daylight and tungsten bulbs will keep you prepared for most any situation.

If you want to make things even simpler, they make professional lighting that allows you to control how bright the light is, and you can smoothly select the color temperature by twisting a dial to get just the right hue! _(See online index)_

If your camera has a white balancing option on it, this is also a setting that shouldn't be ignored. A lot of DSLR cameras will have presets for white balancing the look of your camera on cloudy days, sunny days, in incandescent lighting inside, and other situations where you can dial the color temp right to where you want it. Setting this accordingly and combining it with a a nicely lit set makes all the difference!

5. <u>Mic Check 1, 2, 1, 2…</u>

Audio…Really the only thing that matters…

Of course I say that facetiously…But think about it — pretty much every video we watch these days has some kind of audio accompanying it, but not all audio has some kind of video. We still buy (*or stream*) music on our mobile devices, our appetites for audiobooks are voracious, and think about how long radio has been around. Even with the proliferation of all the forms of media we consume today, radio — satellite or otherwise — is still kicking like Bruce Lee. Yeah — audio is pretty much the ultimate communication tool, and there are so many different things you can do with it, and it's my favorite "weapon of mass production"!

Also, I want you to think about this…If you went to see a movie at a theater and the sound was terrible, would you go back? Probably not. Why do you suppose, back in the day when surround sound was growing in popularity, theaters used to tout this as one their biggest attractions? Remember all the ads (yes let's call them what they were — ads) THX, Dolby Digital? Today, superior sound has come to be *expected* and is no longer the attraction it once was. People pay for, and *expect* good audio.

I have people tell me all the time, if they find a video on youtube that's kind of crappy but the audio is good, they'll stick around and watch. But if the audio is bad, bye bye! Think about how many times in your own experience on Facebook or Youtube that you've done the same.

What I'm saying here doesn't diminish the importance of video in your media arsenal. You really should strive to have the best of both worlds audio and video. However, if you're just getting started with producing your own content, your priority should be better audio.

So now that we've _**firmly**_ established that audio is where it's at — tongue-in-cheek — how should you think about it in terms of your media? How you sound should be among one of your top concerns. And I'm not referring to you being able to "talk good." What I mean is how intelligible is your audio itself? How full, clear, and crisp does it sound?

Here's what you should be thinking about:

If you regularly shoot videos for social media or products you develop, and you only use the microphone on your cell phone, or camera — ask yourself why you've never considered anything beyond that…And now CONSIDER IT!

Thinking Like An Audio Engineer:

When you shoot a video of yourself with a regular camera, or a cell phone camera, where do you stand? Usually in front of the camera, right? Usually at some distance away from the camera, right? And if you are using the microphone that is built into the cell phone or camera, where is that microphone located? On the cell phone or camera! Again, where are you standing? At some distance _away_ from the camera — _away_ from the microphone!

While some of you reading this may see this as acceptable, let me give you a few reasons why this should be the exception rather than your norm.

1. Cameras are really good at being cameras — period. This includes the cameras on cell phones. The microphone that's included on these devices is so you can at least capture _some_ kind of sound with the videos you shoot. They are not included to capture professional grade audio. So already you're at a disadvantage, capturing audio that is inferior in quality.

2. When the microphone is any distance away from you, especially in an "everyday household" setting, you **will** hear the sound of the room in your recording. Many household rooms are not kitted out like pro audio and tv studios, being treated for sound reflections and all. Therefore, no matter how beautiful your room may look on camera, it can still totally *sound* like butt. With your microphone being farther away from you *(because it's on your camera)*, your room can sound like BIG butt! The farther away the microphone is from you, the less it starts to pick up your actual voice and the more it starts to pickup the reflections of the room you're in.

3. Let's not forget the whole reason you're reading this book. You are trying to learn how to effectively wield A/V to represent your brand in the best light possible, to increase your exposure, expand your influence, and grow your revenue. Some of you speakers out there, have positioned yourselves as "executive coaches" or sell yourselves as coaching others "at the highest levels of their organizations" — "high performance coaching," etc. While this all may very well be true, your terrible A/V quality can be a strong indicator and deterrence to potential clients who are seeing and experiencing your media for the first time. C'mon man…first impressions! SET THE TONE — a professional one!

So don't settle for audio that sounds "cheap" — or worse yet, "shortchanged".

At this point, you're probably thinking, "so *what am I supposed to do if I'm not supposed to use the microphone on my camera?!"*

You use it, but you don't use the audio from it in your final product.

Now you're probably thinking, *"If I'm not going to use the audio from that microphone, why record any audio with it at all? Isn't that a waste of time?"*

No, and I'll explain why later on. For now, embrace the thought that you *will* need to invest in a decent microphone. Depending on what kind you get, I'll also strongly advise picking up the needed accessories to maximize the value you get from that microphone. *(Remember? No one magic bullet, no one giant leap.)*

And btw, when I say invest in a "decent" microphone — if I had to put a price on it — that would mean nothing less than $150 at the cheapest just to "get by". *(Talib Kweli, anyone?)*

There's a reason $700 microphones sound like $700 and $30 microphones sound like…well you know…$30. Must you have a $700 microphone? No. Do $700 microphones sound amazing? Just about every time. Before you just go out and buy a microphone though, think about *what* you'll use that microphone for and *how* you'll use it. There are different microphones for different purposes. And of course as with any purchase these days it goes without saying, do your homework, read the reviews.

Quick Recommendations on Mics:

The microphones I list hereafter are great options, but you shouldn't limit your selection only to what I say…Instead use the following information more as a guide to compare other microphones that would be similar to see if you find something that would better suit your needs. If you find something absolutely amazing, let me know…I just might wanna get one for myself! Or, you could just stick with what I recommend if you want to take the easy route.

For all microphones, a specification I like to pay close attention to is the frequency response. When you find this information about a microphone you're interested in, it will most likely look something like this:

40Hz - 16KHz *(these are pretty good numbers by the way!)*

The manufacturer may also provide some type of graphical representation of the frequency response of the microphone too. This is helpful because this will give you an idea of what frequencies may possibly need adjusting in your audio when you're all done recording.

Sometimes you'll have to do a little digging to find this information out about a microphone, maybe even going as far as emailing the manufacturer.

When looking at the frequency response information, remember that the range of human hearing spans roughly from 20Hz (*hertz*) on the low end, all the way up to 20KHz (*kilohertz*) on the high end. As an audio guy, I prefer a microphone that covers as much of this range as possible, because it gives me more information to work with, a bigger diamond with which to start cutting from and turning that audio into a true gem. The smaller the range of the frequency response, the less information there is in the audio to work with.

On the low end, I wouldn't use a mic that has a starting frequency response above 80Hz, and on the high end, nothing less than 16KHz. It won't sound absolutely terrible beyond these numbers, but in my book it won't sound absolutely amazing either.

Now, let's discuss types of uses, and the microphones best suited to handle those situations.

Audio-Only Projects:

If you need to capture audio for audiobooks, and other audio-only programs, like radio interviews, you'll want to get something that can provide a nice "studio" sound. A condenser microphone like the Rode NT1-A would be a great start at an affordable price to get you sounding "crispy" as my friend Cori Briggs, The Builder, would say.

Condenser mics, regularly used in studios around the world, are usually quite sensitive allowing users to capture every nuance of their voice. Most are so sensitive they can "hear" the sound of the air in the room around them. These are excellent additions to your media toolkit.

One thing to be prepared for with pretty much all condenser microphones, is that they usually require an extra 48 volts of power to operate them. This is called phantom power. Pretty much every audio interface or mixer you can buy nowadays provides this extra power. *(More info is (provided on audio interfaces in chapter 7)*

Now if you really must go cheaper than $150, a tried-and-true, practically indestructible workhorse to take a look at would be the Shure SM58. Instead of being a condenser microphone, this is what's known as a *dynamic* microphone. Dynamic mics don't require phantom power, and are usually used in more live settings. For instance, concerts, or live speaking engagements such as when the President of the United States addresses the nation. The two microphones that you see on the Presidential podium, are SM58s. You *can* use dynamic mics in a studio setting just fine. With a model like the SM58 you'll want to keep in mind that it produces a little bit of self-noise so there's that to deal with in your recordings, and in my experience using it, it takes a little more work than a condenser mic to dial in your equalization (EQ) just right, and get the most natural representation of your voice in your recordings. So you'll need a little more experience with audio and using EQ if you go this route.

One other thing about dynamic microphones is that leaving phantom power engaged on your audio interface or mixer can damage some models. The SM58 is fine with phantom power being on or off, but make sure if you get a model different from this that you read the manual to make sure you don't tear up your new microphone before you even get to try it out!

Audio for Video Projects:

If you need to capture professional sound for video work, you may want to look into a lavalier (lav) microphone, or a shotgun microphone. Depending on the look you're going for you may even be able to repurpose your condenser or dynamic mic and save a little coin.

If you absolutely don't want to see a microphone in scene at all, find a place under your shirt to hide a lav, or get a shotgun mic and put it on a stand out of scene.

If you stay pretty stationary in your videos and don't do a whole lot of moving around, your best option will be to use a shotgun microphone such as the Audio-Technica AT8035. Shotguns are great for this kind of work. They're also known as hyper-cardioid microphones — in other words, they are *very* directional. Where ever you point them, they will pick up sound from that direction with a greater focus while rejecting other noises off-axis, meaning to the sides or behind the microphone. They do this to a greater degree than other types of microphones.

Now, if microphones being in the shot don't scare you like the monsters hiding under your bed, then a lav mic is a great option. But hey! If you don't mind the mic in the shot, as I've said before you could even use your condenser or dynamic mic I mentioned earlier and save the money you would've otherwise spent on a lav mic, thereby making your set look cool, and you like you know what you're doing. If you use one of these two options though instead of the lav, you'll have to be aware of where you are in relation to the microphone. If you shift far enough away, you'll hear a difference in the sound with these types of mics.

Which brings me to the beauty of a lav mic. For the most part I've largely not said a whole lot about lavs because there's a lot of ground to cover here. So I'll go into that now.

Lavalier microphones are simple, especially if they are wired. You clip it onto your shirt and go. No matter where you move, the mic is always attached to you in the same spot. So you really don't have to worry about your proximity to the mic as much as you would a condenser or dynamic because your sound should remain pretty consistent. Sony makes a very nice wired lav mic that would be worth checking out. However, there are some things to look out for that you just wouldn't know unless you use lavs on a regular basis, and they can either make your experience with them a dream or nightmare.

Depending on what kind of clothes you wear *(usually heavily starched linen-like materials)* you may pick up a lot of rustling noise from those clothes. For women, big clangy necklaces should be avoided to keep from banging the microphone every time you move. And then too, you have to be deliberate in your choice of where you clip a lav onto yourself or other people to ensure they are heard at all times. (*I discuss this further in the mic techniques I share in chapter 6*)

Usually though, when talking about lavalier microphones, using them wirelessly is what comes to peoples' minds — No strings attached, hands free. And this is why I say lavs can be dreams or nightmares. Once you understand the potential pitfalls of going wireless, you'll be well on your way to looking "BOSS" while you use your wireless lav.

The first thing you need to understand is that when purchasing a wireless microphone of any kind, you're purchasing more than just the microphone — you're purchasing a wireless *system*. So for lavs, this includes the microphone that clips onto you, the transmitter that you clip onto your belt that your microphone plugs into, and the receiver that gets the signal from the transmitter and sends that signal where ever you route it to from there (*mixer, audio interface, etc.*)

You also need to:

- Be aware of the potential for wireless interference and what to do if you encounter any.

- Ensure the wireless system you purchase operates within the range of frequencies designated by the FCC for wireless microphone usage in the U.S. or the frequencies specified by the FCC's counterparts in other countries if you're international.

- Be prepared to spend some money. This is an area you absolutely cannot cheap-out on. Investment minimum for a wireless lav system: $300-$500, at least. $500-$800 recommended!

Brand names I trust for the task — Sennheiser, Shure, Audio-Technica. *(Specific models are listed in the online index)*

So wireless interference…What is it, and what do you do if you encounter any? If you think back to the way we used to work the dial on our radios, trying to get the needle in just the right spot to hear our favorite songs, do you remember what would happen sometimes if there was a neighboring station nearby? You would get interference in your signal. And goodness, don't let somebody bump the antenna out of place! You'd be forever trying to set that thing back in just the right spot!

With wireless microphones, you most likely won't be picking up any "oldies but goodies," but the interference you experience could come in the form of sudden and sporadic white noise in your signal while you are using it, or your audio could simply drop out for a brief moment like someone hit the mute button. Other weird anomalies can occur as well. I once worked a broadcast where the presenters wireless mics made them sound like they were under water! Test and listen for these occurrences coming out of your PA system <u>before</u> your live events, or if you're shooting a video, plug in some headphones and test it out <u>before</u> you hit the record button.

Where you'll usually find that you have more of an interference problem is in bigger cities. You've got more news and radio broadcasting going on and other live events happening all over the place, and a lot of those entities also use wireless microphones somewhere in their workflow. So you'll be competing with these players, along with other individuals like yourself vying for bandwidth on the frequency spectrum. And in case you aren't getting what I'm saying yet…the frequency spectrum is *finite,* space is limited on it.

So what do you do if you are getting interference? Well this is part of the reason you should invest the extra cash into your wireless system. Some of the options that come with the extra money are changeable channels. Most wireless systems will have "banks" of channels. Usually the more expensive systems have more of these banks and channels to choose from. Having more channels gives you a better chance at finding a frequency on the spectrum with no interference, thereby enhancing the quality of your audio, ergo your show. The other cool thing about most of the newer wireless systems is that they have the ability to scan for the best possible frequency to use in any given area and lock into that channel and be ready for use within seconds. All of this being done with a push of a button. Having this automatic tuner will suffice in most cases.

However, if you really want to play it safe and get super technical with it, they make separate devices called spectrum analyzers that "sniff" out frequencies that are in use where ever you might be, and give you a visual representation of those frequencies. By having something like this you can *see* exactly where you can tune your wireless system to, thereby avoiding any interference. A nifty little device that does this on the cheap is the RF Explorer 3G. Just know, that I'm a "better safe than sorry" kind of guy which is why I shared this little tidbit with you, however, this would most likely be overkill unless you're a person who works heavily down in the nitty-gritty of media production like myself. It's just nice knowing what's out there, y'know?

One of the key things to know when operating wirelessly is the range of frequencies you should be operating in which are designated by the FCC. It's illegal to operate wireless microphones tuned to frequencies designated for other types of communication, like cellular towers for example. The frequency range the FCC has designated for wireless microphones is 470 MHz - 608 MHz. All of the newer wireless systems sold in the United States are already made to operate at a certain bank of frequencies within this range. If you plan to buy used equipment, don't get burned...verify the operating frequency range.

> **_NOTE:_** *the frequencies discussed in this book are for the United States. Different countries may have different operating frequencies. Find out what agencies designate these frequencies in other countries and then buy/rent accordingly.*

If you notice in all of this microphone speak, I didn't mention any headset mics, did I? That's because I personally don't care for the sound quality of the microphones in those units. Unless you're getting one of those nicer ESPN sports announcer type of headsets with really great sounding mics, or something really nice like the Countryman E6, I'd stay away from these — especially the USB ones. I see so many people using those cheap USB headset microphone combinations that you can buy from any electronics store, but if you look at the frequency response of most of those, you'll understand why I prefer not to use them. A lot of them cut everything off below 100Hz, and above 12-16 KHz leaving your voice not sounding as full and crisp as it could be. Those things are fine for working with clients one on one or Skyping with family or things like that, but remember that the quality of your sound and video is part of your brand. So invest in a nice mic and a pair of professional headphones. Save the cheaper headset for another occasion.

I'd also be a little hesitant about recommending USB microphones to anyone either. Some of it is due to personal preference for the tried and true XLR connector, which has been around for forever and really isn't going anywhere, but some more compelling reasons for me are these questions:

What will you do with your microphone when USB is no longer the connection of choice for computers? Computers change overnight. Think about the way printers used to connect to computers before USB came along. Apple is already trying to change the USB port with it's latest lineup of Macs having USB-C installed on them.

Even if you get a USB microphone that also has the XLR connector built-in, what do you do with your microphone, if the manufacturer stops supporting the drivers that allow it to run on your computer? What if the mic has firmware that regularly needs updated, and that somehow gets corrupted rendering your microphone unusable? What does that mean for your microphone?

And what about the components inside of your USB microphone? Essentially what a USB microphone is, is a microphone *and* an analog-to-digital converter in one. Which means your microphone is taking your real-world, analog voice and turning it into ones and zeros on your computer. Not all analog-to-digital converters are created equally, and sometimes, even though the microphone part of a USB mic may be good, manufacturers may not use the best converters. So now, your USB microphone has an "achilles heel" and doesn't sound as good as it should.

These are some of the reasons I prefer to use regular microphones, and leave all my analog-to-digital converting to a high-quality interface. Components that only have one job, instead of multiple, are usually pretty good at doing that *one* job.

With a regular XLR microphone you pretty much only have to worry about it not working if you physically break it. Other than that, it will *always* work. Call me old fashioned, but these are some of the things that cross my mind, and cause me to hesitate every time someone asks me about getting a USB microphone. If you decide to go this way, do your research and future-proof yourself by getting a model that still let's you directly connect an XLR cable to it just in case.

So that should give you an idea of the type of microphones you can look at for your media production. If you produce both audio-only and video content, owning multiple microphones may be in your future. And especially, if you're asking people to pay for that content you should definitely invest in quality gear and training like this book to help you grow your skills and get your future clients to get serious about working with you.

6. <u>Inception</u>

If you've seen the movie *Inception* then you'll know what I mean when I say, this is the part where this becomes a "dream within a dream." We're gonna take it to a deeper level with microphones and talk technique — basic microphone placement, tips and tricks, and a few accessories. Knowing which microphones to use is one thing — *how* to use those microphones is another. So here we go!

Condenser Mics:

Placement is pretty straightforward with these once you get them on a stand. Inside the capsule of the microphone itself, behind the wired mesh part of the mic, is a part called the diaphragm. The diaphragm is flat and circular in shape, like a large coin. To illustrate…Imagine holding up a quarter. If I told you to speak to the "heads" side of the coin, you would know that means you would be speaking directly to the side with George Washington's face on it. You wouldn't turn the coin so that you were speaking to the edge of it, nor would you turn the coin so that the tales side of it faces you. For some condensers, there is a "heads and tales," in other words, a certain side of it that you should speak into. Some condensers only pick up sound from one side of the diaphragm and do not give you the option to switch up your pickup pattern. Don't worry if yours is that way. This is a "nice-to-have" feature in the audio world. You'll just want to read your instruction manual to get familiar with the pickup pattern of your microphone to ensure you are speaking into the right side of it.

Earlier, I mentioned investing in the extra accessories to get the most out of your microphone for your projects. Because condensers are so sensitive, one of those accessories I highly recommend would be a shock mount. Shock mounts work by suspending your condenser mic in a cradle that's held in place by a system of elastic bands. These elastic bands then become the only point by which your microphone is physically connected to the stand, thereby the only connection to the rest of the physical world with all it's unwanted low-end energy. This is key because the bands absorb much of that unwanted energy that travels through the microphone stand, into your microphone, and ultimately into your recording. This unwanted energy can come from you accidentally bumping the mic stand, footsteps from you shifting your weight during recording, adjusting your mic during recording or a live broadcast, etc. Believe me, having a shock mount is a worthwhile investment.

Something else that would take your sound quality up a notch would be to use a windscreen, also known as a pop filter. Just imagine how every word you speak that has a "P" in it sounds without something to block that added wind from hitting the diaphragm of the microphone — pretty crappy! *(try saying that last phrase into your microphone without a windscreen and you'll hear what I mean)*

That burst of air that hits the microphone every time you speak a word with a "P" or a "B" in it is known as a plosive. Hearing plosives, in speech on videos posted to Youtube and Facebook, gets really old really fast.

As far as buying all of this nice gear, back in the day *(like 3 years ago…)*, it used to be that you had to buy your mic, shock mount, and windscreen all separately. Now, more and more companies are matching their mics with shock mounts, and usually the shock mounts have windscreens already built-in! So take a look around at Amazon.com to find some of these bundles. If you want to save the time of looking around and figuring out what to get, this is yet another reason I recommend the Rode NT1-A. Rode provides this kit at a reasonable price. The only thing you should need after buying it, is a good mic stand to hold it all.

I won't go into detail on dynamic mics because the concepts are pretty much the same for them. Find a good shock mount and pop filter for your model and you're good to go!

Another worthwhile investment, especially when it comes to audio-only projects is a good microphone reflection filter. I say "good" because there are a lot of cheap ones out there, and even a lot of the good ones are poorly designed at best. In fact there's really only one reflection filter I feel I can *strongly* recommend. That's the Aston Microphones Halo Reflection Filter. First off, this filter is very light weight compared to the others. Second, it's design allows for it to be balanced very well on your microphone stand. A lot of other professional filters are so heavily weighted, and designed to sit so far forward or back that it actually causes your stand to tip over. I've read many a review on these where people lost good microphones from their stands falling over — no thanks! A third reason I really like this filter is because the manufacturer addressed something that always concerned me with all the other filters. Other filters only wrap around the sides and rear of the microphone, but my question has always been, "what about the space *above* and *below* the microphone as well? Aston has designed their filter to provide the most coverage I've seen to date, and the material it's made out of really does a great job at minimizing unwanted reflections from the rest of your room. There are some filters out there that completely encapsulate your microphone in foam, but having watched videos and read reviews, I would consider these models ineffective…at least for now.

Once you have a reflection filter, if you have a condenser microphone with a selectable pickup pattern, there's a really nice technique you can apply for even cleaner sound. *(The Rode NT2-A microphone is the "big brother" to the NT1-A — it has a selectable pickup pattern).* If you switch the microphone into the bi-directional pickup pattern, *(this is the shape that looks like the figure 8)* the microphone will pick up sound from both the front and rear of the diaphragm, while rejecting sound from the sides. Being that your microphone is inside the reflection filter, though, means that the microphone will really only pick up sound from one side of the diaphragm. This technique allows you to achieve even cleaner recordings! This is because the other patterns on the microphone — omnidirectional, and cardioid — either allow sound to be captured from all sides, or from the front and the sides. Not so with the figure 8!

Shotgun Mics:

Right off the bat, I want to make sure that the shotgun mic you get has the three-pronged XLR connector on the end of it, and not a cheap cable already built-in with a 1/8" sized jack on the other end *(in case you don't know what an 1/8" jack is, that's the same size jack as most consumer headphones — think about Apple's EarPods before they went wireless with their AirPods)*. There are shotguns made like this that are intended to be plugged directly in to cameras. These have their uses, but not for what I'm talking about in this book.

You'll find a lot of people will attach shotguns right on to their cameras and point it at themselves while delivering their lines to the camera. Still others will put them on a stand, lower them out of the bottom of the frame, and point them upward toward their mouth. However, lots of people, including myself prefer to put the shotgun on a stand, raise them up above the talent — just out of the top of the frame, and point them downward toward the talent.

While there's nothing "wrong" with the first two approaches, I'll tell you why these aren't my "go-to" methods. Think back to the hard reflective surfaces I mentioned in chapter 3. If you're shooting videos in a controlled environment, such as your home, there's a possibility you already have carpet — a *non*-reflective surface — on the floor of the room you're shooting in. If you don't have carpet, it's a simple fix — just get some thick blankets and throw them down over the floor *(moving blankets work better than regular blankets — see online index)*. Unless your framing on the camera is a head-to-toe shot, which is rare for most people, you most likely won't be seeing the floor in your video. So by flying the shotgun in from above, you're already saving a few steps or keeping them to a minimum when it comes to treating your room for sound. Just go ahead and try throwing blankets up on your bare, reflective ceiling while pointing the microphone upward towards you…yeah didn't think so…hello *gravity* my old friend, right?

Ok, so why don't I like attaching the shotgun microphone to the camera and pointing at me? You probably think you already know what I'm going to say…"because of the hard, flat, reflective walls behind me, right?" Exactly! But that's only part of what I have to say about this. The other part of it is that depending on how long your shotgun mic is, you may also see it in frame on your camera. If you already know to be on the lookout for this, then you should also know it will take time to look for the right-sized shotgun mic that will work with your camera so this problem doesn't occur. And then, getting back to those hard, flat, reflective walls behind you — they're most likely part of your "set," right? Which also means they are in frame, you can see them in your shot. When it comes time to treat that part of your room for sound so you can make the "attach-your-mic-to-your-camera" method sound better, how are you going to make thick blankets on the wall fit in with the rest of your decor? Even with professional sound dampening material you'll have to find creative ways to make that work with the rest of your set. Which means that's just more time taken away from getting your message out to the masses.

And if you're thinking of skipping out on treating your room for sound, think again. If you've spent the money that you *should* on a decent microphone, you <u>will</u> hear the sound of your room in your recordings if it isn't treated. Your audio <u>will</u> lack that professional quality. It's also much harder to deal with the sound of the room in post-production and editing than it is if you just take the time up front to control your environment at the time of capturing your audio in the first place. (*Again, see my "Good Sound Keeping" Checklist in the index for further tips!*)

Fortunately for me, my videos are about getting better audio at home so having sound dampening material in my shot only helps my cause. You like my shameless plug on my video series? While I'm at it, I might as well tell you, you can go check it out at www.facebook.com/ClefToneGrooves — don't judge.

> <u>*Note:*</u> *When I talk about treating your room for sound, I'm referring to a household bedroom style/home office type of room. Not large open spaces. Bedrooms/home offices usually sound pretty horrible especially if not tamed with a little sound dampening material.*

Another thing I don't like about attaching to the camera is the distance. Remember? We discussed this in the last chapter. While the shotgun microphone can easily pick up what you say, it's still attached to the camera which will most likely be further away from you than where the shotgun mic *could* be positioned when suspended above you. Don't get me wrong, there are times when this method would be the way to go, but standing still in a controlled environment is not one of them...there's a better way. So save yourself the hassle, buy a stand to hold your shotgun mic and fly it in from above. And one more thought on my preferred method, depending on your head room, flying in from above usually gets the shotgun the closest to the source of audio *(you)* out of all the methods I've discussed, and thereby gets you the optimal sound.

There is one thing I recommend being on the lookout for when flying the shotgun in from above. Make sure the microphone doesn't cause any shadows on you, or anywhere else that is noticeable on your set. This can happen depending on how you have you and your set lit. I've made this mistake a time or two — happens to the best of us. And another tip is getting brightly colored electrical tape, yellow or hot pink or something. If your shotgun mic came with a black foam windscreen *(most do)*, slip that onto the mic and then at the very end of that windscreen that will be pointed towards you, take a strip of that electrical tape and wrap it around the circumference of the foam. When you're trying to figure out if your microphone is still in scene or not, this brightly colored tape at the end of that foam will stand out like a soar thumb, which will let you know your mic is in the shot. From there, you simply raise the mic up a bit so that it's just out of frame. You want the mic as close to you as possible, but still just out of the frame of the camera.

One last tip about shotgun mics in general is that the longer the shotgun mic is, the tighter the pickup pattern will be, and on the flip side, the shorter the shotgun, the wider the pattern. To illustrate what I mean, think of when you shine a flashlight on a wall. When you move closer to the wall, the light on the wall covers less surface area. That light on the wall is like your pickup pattern on your microphone. So if you have a pretty long shotgun microphone, you may need to back it off of you just little bit to allow room for any shifting you may do in the video while you deliver your message, otherwise when you shift you may go outside the pickup pattern, and you'll be able to hear the difference in sound immediately.

Lavalier Microphones:

Earlier I mentioned that shotgun microphones pickup patterns are "hyper-cardioid". Well lavs come in two flavors when it comes to pickup patterns. You can get one that's omnidirectional, or you can get one that's cardioid (not to be confused with *hyper*-cardioid). Don't let these terms intimidate you. Simply put, pickup patterns are what directions these microphones pick up sound from, and what directions they reject sound from. Do a search on google for images to these different pickup patterns and you'll see that cardioid is slightly in the shape of a heart *(if looking at a 2D image)*, hence the name "cardioid". You'll see that an omnidirectional pickup pattern looks like a sphere *(if looking at 3D images)*. These diagrams represent how those microphones "hear" the environment around them.

So let me give you some instances where you would want to think about having either a cardioid lav vs. an omnidirectional lav.

Scenario 1: Let's say you're on location at a conference somewhere. You've found someone you want to interview on video, and you only have one lav mic. Being that the omnidirectional mic picks up sound from every direction, this would be the one I choose. Bring your interviewee in close, and clip your lav onto the lapel of your jacket that is closest to them. That way you should be able to pick both of you up in your video. You'll most likely hear the noise of others at the conference in the background so you may need to move away from the crowd a little bit to make sure the two of you are heard loud and clear.

Scenario 2: If you're doing a live speaking gig and you're using sound reinforcement, I would go with a cardioid lav. Why? Because this microphone will be less susceptible to feedback.

> **Note:** *Feedback is that nasty squealing sound you hear come out of your speakers when you walk in front of them with a microphone. What's happening is that the speakers are outputting the sound that the microphone is picking up. However at the same time, the microphone is picking up the sound of what the speakers are putting out. So in effect you are getting a loop that feeds into itself causing what's known as a feedback loop. So the noise keeps reinforcing itself, and gets louder and louder.*

What makes cardioid lavs less susceptible to feedback vs. omnidirectional lavs, is that unlike omnidirectionals, cardioids reject sound from certain directions, focusing more on picking up sound from where they are pointed — kind of like shotgun mics, but with a lesser degree of focus. I still wouldn't walk in front of any speakers with one but having a cardioid lav should definitely make much less feedback noise, if any during live speaking engagements — that, and proper placement of your PA speakers. There's a whole science to speaker placement as well, but some basics are, don't set up any speakers behind you at any live gigs. Place them somewhere in front of you like the edge of the stage, pointed at your audience and away from you.

Scenario 3: When you're shooting videos in a controlled environment such as your home, either microphone would do just fine, however I would still lean a little more towards the cardioid microphone simply because of it's tighter pickup pattern. There is less opportunity for any unwanted noise to bleed into your recording.

When putting on a lav microphone, a good thing to think about is where you'll be facing most of the time. If you'll be facing the camera straight ahead, then the best place to clip it on would be as close to the middle of your chest as possible. If you'll be interviewing someone, then you'll want to cheat the lav towards the side of your chest closest to where the other person will be standing — kind of like what I mentioned earlier in scenario 1. That way, whether you look at the person or look to camera, your audio quality will remain consistent. If your lav is clipped to the left, but you're constantly looking to the right for the interview, you'll notice a difference in your sound quality, especially if you alternate between speaking to camera, and speaking to your interviewee — NOT PROFESH!

As for how high or low you should place the microphone, think about if you were wearing a button down shirt. A good spot is right between the second and third button from the top, towards the top of your heart.

And, while we're talking about button down shirts, this would also be a good time to discuss wardrobe when wearing a lav mic. As an audio engineer, I find I'm presented the most challenges when it comes to women's attire. Don't get me wrong ladies…you have some pretty sweet clothes. But those sweet clothes rarely seem to have a good spot to clip a lav mic onto. Many of the female talent I work with will show up wearing really loose, frilly scarves, or they'll have a shirt that is cut so low, that by the time you get the mic to the center of their torso, the mic is placed way lower than that second and third button. If you clip it at the height I recommend on a shirt like that, the mic winds up way off to the side because of how wide the neckline on the shirt is. Other times, female talent will wear something with no place to clip the microphone to, but their collar of their top. I can't tell you how annoying this is! I realize that part of this is due to lack of knowledge, so after having read this book, consider yourself knowledgeable! So let me just go ahead and *strongly advise* you on what you *should* wear. Here is my ask *(and this applies to male talent too)*:

If you know that you'll be wearing a lavalier microphone at some point throughout your day, dress for it. If you know that you will be using a microphone but you aren't sure what kind it will be, ask well ahead of time so there are no surprises. If you find out it's going to be a lav, then ladies a nice pant suit or skirt with a button down would be awesome, guys a nice suit, or at the very least a button down shirt.

Even if the buttons only go part of the way down like a polo shirt, that's better than having no buttons, because now you have the best options of where you can put the lav, and it's so much easier to hide the extra slack of the wire under your shirt to give a clean, professional, polished appearance.

Wearing a shirt with no buttons, like a crewneck, means you'll wind up clipping the lav to your collar. While it'll pick you up just fine, esthetically it just looks tacky, especially if the clip for the lav mic is one that doesn't swivel…now you just have a lav mic clipped sideways onto your collar, and to me that just doesn't like right, it doesn't look "clean". Personally, I keep clips in my audio kit that can swivel $360°$ so I can at least point the mic upward in the cases where I have to clip it onto someone's collar.

Now, I've spent all this time focusing on the microphone, and I haven't even mentioned the transmitter yet. So let's talk about that. As I mentioned in the preceding chapter, when most people use lavs, they want to be wireless. In order to do that, your mic has to be plugged into a wireless transmitter, also known as a body pack. That transmitter has to stay with you, somewhere on your body. You need a place to either clip it onto, or a pocket to put it in. So ladies, if you wear dresses that zip up from behind and you have no pockets, or not even a belt to clip the transmitter onto, just be prepared to hold that thing in your hand the whole time while you're speaking. At that point, you'd be better off holding a handheld microphone. But really, bottom line, before I put too many other ideas in your head, just wear a button down with a pant suit or skirt, and all these problems go away really fast. Sorry if this suggestion cramps your style, but then again, it's all about getting your message out in a professional way right? Do it for the message — and your future potential clients!

There's one more thing I like to do before putting a lav on someone. I always loop a little bit of the cable through the clip on the mic itself. This helps relieve a little stress on the point where the cable connects to the microphone as well as provides a bit of shock absorption if the cable were to get tugged by any part of your wardrobe, or by the transmitter accidentally coming loose and falling off your body.

Now here's a bit of "nice-to-have" information…Different microphone manufacturers make proprietary connectors for the transmitters in their wireless offerings. You'll need to know about this if you ever decide to upgrade your lav mic to a better quality model. If you have a Sennheiser wireless transmitter, you'll want to look for lavs designed to fit a Sennheiser transmitter. If you have a Shure wireless transmitter, you'll need to look for lavs designed to fit a Shure transmitter.

Most lavs that come with wireless systems are your cheaper ones of the manufacturer's lineup…unless you've spent a good amount of money for your wireless system, chances are you may have one of their cheaper microphones. Don't get me wrong, there's nothing wrong with that. For the most part these mics sound pretty good, and do a great job. However if you ever get a chance to hear what a more expensive model microphone sounds like compared to your starter lav mic, you'll be asking yourself the same question people ask themselves about the cell phone, *"how did we ever live without it?!"* A couple highly recommended brands to look into would be Countryman lavs, and DPA lavs *(see online index)*. The only way I can best describe the sound of these microphones for you is that they sound "transparent". There seems to be very little coloration in the sound of the audio these microphones pick up. They put out one of the truest representations of your voice that I've ever heard. You don't have to do a whole lot of equalization to make these sound good. These are also on the more expensive side too, and this is only for the lav microphone itself, not an entire wireless system. Yes, I mean we're literally talking about only the mic and cable that plug into your body pack, but man if you can swing it, these mics are so worth it!

And that's it for technique, but I have yet another level to take you to, where all of this will really come together and help you get a whole lot closer to that professional level media production. A dream within a dream, *within a dream*?

You follow, I'll lead.

7. <u>Let's Get To The Good Stuff</u>

If there's any part of this book that I'd say I've enjoyed writing the most, it would be this chapter. Sure, I love all the other chapters that came before this one, but they were all like "prerequisites" leading you up to this point here. Without knowing all of the info from the other chapters, you wouldn't benefit nearly as much from reading this one. Many of you reading this book, who have never done things the way I suggest, might look at all of the first 6 chapters as a lot of work. And you're right. It takes serious work to achieve something of quality! You're probably wondering what's the payoff here? Why go to all this trouble with things like matching color temperature in my lighting, buying a professional microphone, scouting my home for an ideal location to shoot, throwing sound treatment around the room I want to shoot in, etc…WHY AM I DOING ALL OF THIS??!!!

Because now that you have all of these little details working together, this chapter is where it all starts to come together, and you really start to see the potential of your final product. Remember, it's these *little* things that add up to *BIG* results. These are the secrets that will set your quality apart from other speakers and coaches who just don't understand the influence, the importance that professionally recorded media has in and on your branding and marketing. Sadly many refuse to understand, and they pay the price for it.

In a way, this reminds me of the televised debate between John F. Kennedy and Richard Nixon. Kennedy understood the importance of media, looking good on camera, even going the extra mile and getting his makeup done for the event. Sure we think of doing makeup for television as a normal thing now, but back then, this was new. This was the first televised Presidential debate! Because Kennedy knew the importance of appearance, with his makeup on he looked cool, calm, and collected — Presidential. Nixon had forgone the makeup and by the end of the debate looked pretty beat with all that sweat all over his face. We all know that history fell in Kennedy's favor, and many say this televised debate was the nail in the coffin that helped catapult him into the Presidency. Kennedy closed the deal. So don't be like Nixon…Make sure you understand the influence, and the importance that media can have on your branding and marketing — professionally recorded media. Then go the extra mile and take care of business, so you can close more deals!

With that said, this chapter will deal specifically with video, capturing your audio for it, and what to do with that audio once it's captured. I'll also uncover the gear behind the microphone that will help you achieve that professional quality that so many people are lacking today.

Ok, so you've shifted your mindset, you've got your script or outline in mind for what you want to say, you've identified the best location to shoot your video that will complement your message, you have it lit perfectly so the light flatters you and your set, you've identified the type of microphone you'd like to use, and now you've properly applied the techniques I've recommended to use that particular microphone to its fullest potential…What comes next?

It's time to prepare your audio gear so you can finally press the record button! Your microphone needs *something* to plug into. And for that task I recommend 1 of 2 options. You can either pickup a a portable digital audio recorder, or you can grab an audio interface that connects to your computer. Either method has it's advantages, both work extremely well for getting the quality you need. So as in previous chapters, let me give you the rundown on which option may be right for you.

Here is what's so cool about portable digital recorders — THEY'RE PORTABLE! These devices are usually handheld in size and pack a lot of helpful features into one very handy device. They're great for recording audio for videos just about anywhere, and don't take up a lot of space in a carry-on bag if you spend a lot of time in airplanes like I do. Even if you don't, it's still nothing to throw one of these bad boys in a go-bag along with your mic and camera, and take off on the double.

Portable digital recorders also have built-in microphones that sound much better than those on cell phones and cameras. Most also come with a hot-shoe mount that will allow you to attach it to your camera. This is especially helpful when you want to keep a small footprint.

But really, as far as using a portable digital recorder, the main features to look for when purchasing are:

- it has a couple of 3-pronged XLR inputs on it,

- it provides phantom power so you can run just about any mic on it,

- it can do sample rates as high as at least 48k *(more on this in a minute)*.

Outside of this, every other feature is pretty much icing on the cake. Sometimes you can catch a model with these features on Amazon for less than $150, but on average I would expect to spend at least that much for one, if not more.

A really nice feature that has come in handy on mine quite a bit is that it has built-in wifi! It puts out its own wifi signal that my phone can connect to, and then I can control the recorder through an app on my phone. For me this has become handy because of working in a small space where I shoot my videos. Sometimes it gets a little tricky to move around my set without disturbing my lighting or cables that I've run to different destinations. So now instead of having to get up to push the record button on my recorder, I can just do it from my phone in my hand! If you're curious to know what model recorder I have, see the online index.

Keep in mind if you use a portable digital recorder, that you'll just have an extra step of transferring your files to a computer to sync them up with your video. This isn't hard, but it still takes time. The other thing you'll always need to stay on top of, is making sure you have extra batteries. It always seems that at the most inopportune times, I run out of juice on my recorder, and then I have to stop to change batteries. So it's just good practice to have fresh batts on standby, ready to go.

Before you start recording anything with your digital recorder, you'll also want to set your recording format to WAV 24-bit. If you see an option that says WAV "PCM", or "uncompressed", go for that. Do NOT record in MP3 format or any other compressed format your recorder may offer. These are dirty words to an audio engineer if you tell them you recorded your stuff in a compressed format. WAV is king! Starting with the highest quality possible is imperative.

I mentioned earlier that one of the three main features your recorder should have is the ability to record audio with at least a 48k sample rate. When working with video, it has become the standard to record your audio with the sample rate set to 48k. If you are capturing audio for a video that will end up on an ultra high def format such as Blu-ray, it has become the accepted standard to record your audio with your sample rate set at 96k. Other than that you can pretty much do your videos at 48k for the most part, no problem. You may have seen sample rate information in the past and just not have known it. If you've ever looked at details for songs you've downloaded on your computer you may have seen "44,100". You may have even seen "48,000" for other audio files you have. This is referring to sample rate. Using 48k is better for syncing up your audio with your video. And although, most people can't hear the difference, it is a bit higher quality than CD-quality audio which is always set at a sample rate of 44.1k.

> **<u>Note:</u>** *If you know what frame rate is to video, then you know what sample rate is to audio. If you don't know what these*

are, it's pretty much how many "snapshots" your device is taking per second during recording. The higher these numbers are set, frames or samples, the more "snapshots" are taken, the more information there is to work with in your video and audio in post. For video, setting a higher frame rate, like 60 frames per second, means having the ability for getting nicer, buttery, silky-smooth, slow motion — If you're into that sort of thing. If you don't slow-mo your footage at that frame rate, it will look very "newsy" and "real", having less of that motion blur that you are use to seeing in TV shows and movies that give them a "softer" look than nightly news. If you do want more of that softer blurred look, you'll need a camera that can shoot at 24 framers per second with the shutter speed set to 48, or as close to 48 as possible. All of this is a whole other subject for you to read up on some time.

For audio, having a higher sample rate means you'll capture more samples per second of the audio that you're recording. So 48k, is more information to work with than 44.1k, and 44.1k is more than 22k. So in effect the quality of your sound is affected by changing this number. Your file sizes will also be affected by this number as well…the higher the number, the bigger your files will be — something to keep in mind when shopping for an SD card. I recommend nothing less than a card with 32 GB of space on it — at least.

Some recorders may give you options to capture audio all the way up to 96k, or even 192k. Outside of the Blu-ray standards mentioned earlier, there are plenty of debates out there about recording at these higher sample rates, and if you can really hear the difference after a certain point…I'm not going to get into all that. Just know that for the purpose of shooting video, go with 48k, 24-Bit WAV. For audio-only projects, 44.1k and WAV 24-Bit will be just fine. If you plan to burn the audio to a CD, you'll need to convert the file to 44.1k, WAV 16-Bit. If you foresee your audio-only projects making their way into videos down the road, record them at 48k, then make a copy of that file and down convert it to 44.1k (*See the online index for a good sample rate converter)*. This way you'll have files ready for both video and audio distribution.

If you decide to go the audio interface route instead of the portable digital recorder route, this is another great solution to capturing audio for your videos. Just like with using your portable recorder, be sure to change your settings in your audio software so that you're recording all audio at 48k, WAV 24-Bit. All software is a little bit different whether you use free audio software like Audacity or Garage Band, or higher-end paid software like PreSonus Studio One, or Apple's Logic. Consult the manual for the software you use to find out how to do this.

A great plus to using an audio interface is that it's already connected to your computer. This means you'll be recording your audio straight into your favorite audio software and you can make any adjustments to the sound right off that bat, no transferring of files necessary. I really like this method because I like to sweeten my audio a little bit before syncing it up with my footage. I may add sound effects at certain parts, I always throw some EQ on it, and sometimes I'll do a little extra. You can't do all that only using a portable recorder. The only downside of using an audio interface is that it's not quite as mobile as a digital recorder being that you'd have to carry the interface and a laptop around in addition to your other gear. This means having extra weight to carry around. However, they make some interfaces small enough that you can still get around fairly easily with them. *(See the online index for some recommendations)*

Because they connect to your computer, you can use audio interfaces for other things besides just recording your audio. For instance, you can do broadcasts online and use your really nice microphone through your interface so your viewers could hear you with awesome sound quality. And if someone wants to interview you for a radio program, you can now use your interface and microphone to sound like you're right there in the studio with them, rather than phoning it in all the time! Talk about a huge boost in your sound quality, professionalism, and your brand!

While it isn't really prevalent yet, except for some high-dollar portable recorders, manufacturers are starting to make some digital recorders that also act as audio interfaces when connected to your computer. A company by the name of Sound Devices offers this with their MixPre series of field recorders. I've gotten to use their mixers countless times on many productions and the sound they capture is just gorgeous! Hop on youtube and search around for some videos that show you audio tests with their MixPre mixers and you'll hear what I'm talking about. A good set of headphones will help the average listener discern the quality even better. This will become the norm in the near future, I'm sure of it!

For either your digital recorder or your audio interface, you'll want to set the recording levels so that you don't clip the meters. Most software, or devices have peak light indicators that light up when your levels are too hot. Usually the color of this light or indicator is red. So test your levels before you get started by delivering a little bit of your message as if you had gone live. Watch your meters as you do this. If you see these indicators light up, it's time to turn down your recording level a bit. As a general rule of thumb, the highest level you'd want those meters to hover around during your delivery, is about 75% of the entire meter.

> **<u>Note:</u>** *Clipping is when your audio signal is overdriven. In digital audio, that's when your levels reach 0dB or higher. While there are some things you can do to sort of work with clipped audio, it comes at a price. So it's better to never have clipped your audio at all. You can always turn your audio up, but once it's clipped, you can't turn it back down. So err on the side of caution and record at lower levels if you think you'll run the risk of clipping your audio for any given recording. Some digital recorders offer a "dual mode" recording feature that allows you to record your audio at the*

level you set, but it also records a "safety" copy of the same audio at a lower level, like -6 dB. This way if you clip your audio on the main file, you have the safety recording as a backup.

This next tip is a super powerful one that will up your quality tremendously. Throughout this chapter, you've heard me talk about syncing audio up with video. This all has to do with the question I left you with back in chapter 5.

What do you do if you aren't supposed to use the audio straight from your camera microphone?

Very briefly, I answered this by saying that you "use the audio from your camera, just not in your final product." Then I deferred sharing the details to a later time. *Now* is that later time.

So why record audio on your camera at all? Because it's a means to an end.

Not only will you press the record button on your camera, but now you'll also be pushing "record" on your audio device as well. Press record on your camera and your audio device simultaneously, or as close to the same time as possible. Once your recording is started on both your camera and audio device, stand in front of the camera, bring your hands up where the camera can see them and clap a few times. Clap loud enough so that your camera mic and your professional mic pick up that sound. Wait a few seconds, smile at the camera, then start delivering your message. Do this all in the same take as your claps. Every time you stop recording on one device, stop recording on the other. Every time you start a new recording, do your claps as I've just described.

By clapping, you'll cause a waveform to appear in both your camera audio files, and the audio files recorded by your professional microphone that have a very short duration, but stand out in loudness so you can see it in editing later. You might clip one of your microphones, but don't worry about it in this case. You won't use any of this in your final product. You'll edit this out later.

Once you stop recording, import your audio file from your professional microphone into your video editing software. From there, look at your audio from both your pro mic and your camera. Look for the part where you did the clapping. You'll see those waveforms from your claps at the beginning of your files. In your video editing software, slide your audio from your pro mic until the claps in that audio match the audio from your camera as closely as possible. You should be able to get them extremely close, if not exactly matched. Now play back your video and watch yourself clap. See if the sound matches up with the motion you see in the video. Skip ahead and see how your sync is looking when you're delivering your message. Hint: it shouldn't look like one of those old kung fu movies when the character on screen starts speaking 5 seconds after their English voiceover line was delivered! If the sync looks good, turn down the audio from your camera and leave the audio in place from your professional microphone, and now you have audio that is out of this world!

What you've just done is pretty much what they do when making movies. Often times when they start a new scene you'll see that clap board on screen and hear someone yell *"Take 6!"* And they slap that arm down nice and loud. By clapping your hands, you've just done it the more "cost effective" way.

So, I've just described to you the manual way of syncing your audio and video, but a lot of software nowadays, will sync it all for you in just a few clicks of the mouse. I use Apple's Final Cut on my Mac and it does a very good job with syncing audio and video.

Now, if after reading this you're thinking, *"I don't have video editing software, or audio software,"* don't panic…I have all those resources listed for you in the *Video Editing Software* and *Digital Audio Workstation* sections *of the* online index.

So having perfectly synced your audio up with your video, you're ready to edit your video to your heart's content! Cut it together how you want it, play it back and see what all your hard work has brought you. You'll definitely notice a difference! If you've taken the tips from all these chapters and applied them, you should most definitely have a product that you're more than happy to call part of your brand!

8. <u>Lemme Get That Anti-Shine!</u>

Gentlemen, let me talk to you about one last important consideration…It's something that ladies already know well…Knowing how NOT to have a shiny face while on camera. Oh YES — we're gonna talk about some makeup! I called it "anti-shine" in the title of this chapter so you men out there wouldn't freakout and rage-quit my book! I was *really* serious when I said I've worn makeup before!

Think back about my earlier analogy about *then* candidate Kennedy and how he looked cool, calm, collected, even Presidential during his debate with Nixon. Remember what I said he understood the importance of? Looking good on camera. He put that makeup on and went to work becoming the 35th President of the United States.

So know this men — It's truly a manly thing to look your best. It's also a professional thing too!

I've been doing basic makeup and more for TV for nearly 10 years now, and I'm going to share some observations with you that I run into all the time with certain skin tones. Be on the look-out, and address these things if you're a guilty party before firing up that camera.

Keep in mind the whole point of doing makeup is to give you a nice even skin tone with a matte finish. This is one way you *don't* want to shine!

White Dudes

More often than not, when I do makeup on caucasian men, a common thing I have to address is dry facial skin. It seems to be more of a thing with men who are middle-aged or older, but every so often I'll find young caucasian guys as well sporting the "dry-face". I'll find flakes of skin peeling from their cheeks, foreheads, and temples. Another place is also right around the eyebrows. White dudes, I don't know about you, but if I was running around looking dry and crusty like this all the time, I'd head to my local beauty store and pick up a bottle of oil-free moisturizer, or some kind of lotion — at least — and work this into my daily routine after I get out of the shower…So why not do that?! If you're married, PLEASE, stop going out in public embarrassing your spouse like that! That way, maybe you'll only need to do a spot treatment right before you shoot your video.

Now, I'm no dermatologist, but I suspect that lack of moisture in the face may contribute to the next problem I often have to address with caucasian men, especially the older ones. I'm talking about rosacea. If dryness isn't a contributing factor, I certainly don't think it helps! The discoloration caused by all those little, red, spidery looking veins that show up on their cheeks, their noses, foreheads, and even chins. If you suffer from this, concealer is your best friend! Find a shade that matches your skin tone, start with a small amount and only add more as needed. Blend so that you don't see any lines of where the makeup has been applied to your face. You can do your blending with one of those triangular shaped sponges. The key word here is "sheer"! In addition to "sheer," words like "dab," "thin," and "modest" are good to keep in mind. The words "cake," "slather," "dump," or "spread" should not come to your mind when it comes to using makeup as these words would indicate that you have applied too much. Lastly, "lock in" your concealer by dabbing on a thin layer of translucent powder with a powder brush. Don't just powder the areas of your face that have concealer. Cover the whole face, especially the space right between the eyebrows, all of the forehead, and the tip of your nose.

Black Guys

I hope you didn't think you were off the hook! For every white dude that's dry in the face, I find just as many black guys that have more than enough oil on their face to coat the bottom of a frying pan, myself included. Brothas, we can't be on the camera shining like that. If you have oily skin, ya'll know who you are. We've got to tone it down — literally! Go to the store, get some toner, and add this to your daily routine. Something you can find in particular at beauty stores that's great for controlling excess amounts of oil, are oil blotting sheets. If you're cheap, or too embarrassed to go to the beauty store for these little guys, most public restrooms nowadays have those tissue paper toilet seat covers in the stalls. Those work great for this purpose too. Just don't let anyone catch you pressing a toilet seat cover on to your face! I think I'd just rather go to the beauty store in all honesty, but for real those toilet seat covers work great in a pinch!

In addition to controlling your shininess, black guys, you'll want to use concealer in your shade to take care of any blemishes like our fellow white dudes, and then lock it in with some powder so it will last you through the duration of your video. If your complexion is on the lighter side, a thin layer of translucent powder should work fine for you. If you are on the darker side of the "complexion palette," it would be best to find an anti-shine powder in a shade that's as close to the color of your skin as possible. Translucent powder is white in color. Using it on extremely dark skin can cause you to look "ashy". On all dark complexions, using *too much* of it can have the same effect.

Another little note on translucent powder. We mentioned how it can make black people look "ashy." Well, too much on white people can make them look "ghostly." So in some cases, caucasians may want to find powder a little closer to their skin tone as well.

Bald Guys

Yes…you need to put anti-shine on that dome! Other than that, unless you have anything blatantly obvious like a giant scar on your head, I wouldn't worry too much about concealer up there.

For everyone, one other thing that helps your makeup apply better is silicone primer. After you've added any needed moisturizer or removed your excess oil, but before you apply any other makeup, work this into your skin all over your face — remember, sheer! Don't glob this on either.

So this is the order I would apply everything:

1. Moisturizer/Oil blotting sheets

2. Silicone primer with a triangular sponge

3. Concealer for covering blemishes

4. Foundation *(I see this one as optional, but this REALLY helps even out your skin tone)*

5. Lock it all in with a little anti-shine power — the translucent type, or the type that is close to your complexion.

6. When finished with your video, use makeup removal wipes to take it all off, or you can just go around being a beautiful man for the rest of the day!

As for all my other dudes out there, that aren't white, but aren't exactly black either, the list I laid out above also applies to you as well. Just make the adjustments for your skin tone and you're set.

Even though I just generalized whole races in this chapter, there *are* white dudes with oily skin, just as there *are* black guys with dry skin. These were just common observations I often notice. On an individual level you'll just need to take an honest look at your skin and see what might show up on camera and address it — simple.

On a health tip, if you have other people appear in your videos on a regular basis, DON'T share your makeup or brushes with them! This is not sanitary. There's all kinds of details and considerations to keeping your makeup and brushes sanitized, but to make things easier, just make sure the other person has their own makeup.

And gentlemen, one last thing…. If you've done your makeup right, no one watching your videos should be able to tell that you have any makeup on at all. Keep that in mind if you're still hesitant about trying out this "anti-shine" tip.

End Game

Well, I hope you've enjoyed reading this book, as much as I enjoyed writing it. I really hope you learned quite a few things you can take away from this book and apply immediately in your own workflow when creating content for your clients, fans, viewers, and listeners.

As I've stated before, everything in this book is included to help you effectively wield media in a way that will position you, your message, and your brand in the best light — to show you off as the true professional that you are. By following the suggestions I've outlined, it adds more weight to your words when you say you're "an executive coach," or a "high performance coach," or any other attribute you want to be known for.

While this may require investment in some new gear, it'll be well worth it as you see the results on the back end. Think of how many more people seeing your message at *that* time will want to work with you because of your professionalism. You've already invested in yourself when you got this book. So why not seal the deal and invest in the tools that will take you the rest of the way? Upgrading the quality of your audio visual content only means that the stage you command the world's attention from will be far grander than it is now. You'll be setting yourself up for successful outcomes while increasing your exposure, expanding your influence, and growing your revenue.

At the outset of this book, I said something that I think would be an appropriate thought to leave you with now:

The will to prepare is the will to succeed.

SET THE TONE!

<u>Index</u>

…And you thought I was done…how cute.

By now you've probably gotten tired of all those captions in each chapter talking about *"see the index." This* is one of two said indices *loaded* with recourses and information designed to get you up and running quickly on all the topics I cover in the book. You can access the online index for more info on gear and software by going to *www.ClefToneGrooves.com/book-index*. These here will be like your *"treasure chests"*!

Releases:

Ah yes, in the litigious society we've all come to know and hate these days, one of the best things you can do when conducting any business on behalf of your brand is to cover your rear end! As you gain more exposure and expand your brand, and move on to bigger productions, these documents will become more important. However, it never hurts to get in the practice of securing releases while you're small. Building your brand means nothing if someone can take it all away with a single lawsuit. This isn't one of the more glamorous parts of content creation, but it's definitely worth taking the time to make everything "official." Below are some sample releases for the different situations you may find yourself in. These are all good starting points to get you going, but feel free to copy and adjust any of these to your needs.

The first release is a general release form for anyone to sign that's at least 18 years of age and older. This gives you permission to use them in pictures, video, soundbites, by name, etc. for your production.

The next release is a minor release. For those under 18 years of age, you must have their parent or legal guardian sign this to cover you for the same things that the general release affords you — images, video, audio, etc.

The release after that is the location release. If you're doing a video in a place or space that's owned by someone else, chances are they'd like to know about it, and will appreciate you getting permission first.

The next release is an existing materials release. Other people's artwork, literature, music, footage from other events, pictures, and the like are all *existing materials*, and as such should be assumed copyrighted. If you haven't paid a licensing fee to use this material, it's a good idea to try and secure a release from them that gives you the permission to use it in your products and projects.

The last release doesn't really require a signature…This is legal language that you can put on a large display sign and post outside the entrance(s) to one of your events. So for instance, if you've secured a conference space at a hotel or something, this means they've given you control over that space for the amount of time that you are there. During this time is when this signage becomes effective and binding. However, if you have no agreements in place for the space you are using, then the language on this release will not protect you. It has to be posted at the entrance(s) of the space you control/own, even if that control is temporary.

Personal Appearance Release

I give unconditional permission to *COMPANY* ("Company") forever, to shoot photographs and/or video of my image, record my voice, and put the words that I speak down in print, a.k.a. "transcription" ("Material"). Material created will come from: ____

(Event name or multimedia recording project).

Company has the sole right to grant third parties, subsidiaries and other associates up to and including the same rights and permissions granted to Company by this entire agreement.

I give Company complete rights and copyright ownership of the material bearing my image without any limits. I know Company doesn't have to use any of the material, but can choose on its own, without hinderance from anyone, to use them without limits, for promotional purposes, audio/visual works, and display them in any way at any time in the future throughout the universe, and that's fine by me. The Company can also use my name if they want, in association with these materials too because I think Company is awesome. If not, I'm cool. It's not an issue. The Company can use the material repeatedly and perpetually.

Since this is a release, and because I love Company, In legal speak I say, "I will hold Company harmless from any and all claims of libel, slander, and/or invasion of privacy because of said material."

In plain English, the Company has given me their word through this agreement that they will never intentionally slander me or just flat out make me look like a terrible person with this material. Therefore, I will irrevocably waive any and all rights to sue Company for any such claims including but not limited to defamation, slander, libel, and the like.

I agree, my appearance in any material is strictly voluntary, not employment; is not subject to any union or guild collective bargaining agreement, and does not entitle me to wages, salary, unemployment or workers' compensation benefits, or other compensation under any such collective bargaining agreement or otherwise.

I understand and accept the possibility that after signing this agreement, I may discover facts, details, or claims which were unknown or unsuspected at the time this agreement was signed, and had I known at that time may have affected my decision to sign this agreement. I acknowledge and accept that by reason of this agreement, I am assuming any risk of such unknown facts, details, and claims unknown and unsuspected. Once I grant the rights outlined in this agreement, I understand and agree that my decision is irrevocable.

This agreement shall be interpreted under the internal, substantive law of the state of *Company's home state* without regard to the conflicts of law provisions thereof. The parties submit to the exclusive jurisdiction and venue of the state and federal courts located in *Company's home County, State*, and waive any objections that they may have as to jurisdiction or venue in any such courts.

This is the complete and binding agreement between Company and me, and it supersedes all prior understandings and communications, both oral and written, with respect to its subject matter. If any provisions of this agreement are found unenforceable this will not affect the validity or enforceability of any of the remainder of this agreement, which shall be enforced to the maximum extent permitted by law. This agreement cannot be terminated, rescinded or amended, except by a written agreement signed by both Company and me.

I am of lawful age and have read and understand this Personal Appearance Authorization, Assignment, and Release.

Signature: ___________________________________ Date: ______________

Print (Neatly): ____

Full Address:____

Phone: ____

Minor Appearance Release

I give unconditional permission to *COMPANY* ("Company") forever, to shoot photographs and/or video of my child's/ward's image, record their voice, and put the words that they speak down in print, a.k.a. "transcription" ("Material"). My child's/ward's name is ____

Material created will come from: ____
(Event name or multimedia recording project).

Company has the sole right to grant third parties, subsidiaries and other associates up to and including the same rights and permissions granted to Company by this entire agreement.

I give Company complete rights and copyright ownership of the material bearing my child's/ward's image without any limits. I know Company doesn't have to use any of the material, but can choose on its own, without hinderance from anyone, to use them without limits, for promotional purposes, audio/visual works, and display them in any way at any time in the future throughout the universe, and that's fine by me. The Company can also use my child's/ward's name if they want, in association with these materials too because I think Company is awesome. If not, I'm cool. It's not an issue. The Company can use the material repeatedly and perpetually.

Since this is a release, and because I love Company, In legal speak I say, "I will hold Company harmless from any and all claims of libel, slander, and/or invasion of privacy of my child/ward because of said material."

In plain English, the Company has given me their word through this agreement that they will never intentionally slander my child/ward, or just flat out make my child/ward look like a terrible person with this material. Therefore, I will irrevocably waive any and all rights to sue Company for any such claims including but not limited to defamation, slander, libel, and the like.

I agree, my child's/ward's appearance in any material is strictly voluntary, not employment; is not subject to any union or guild collective bargaining agreement, and does not entitle me or my child/ward to wages, salary, unemployment or workers' compensation benefits, or other compensation under any such collective bargaining agreement or otherwise.

I understand and accept the possibility that after signing this agreement, I may discover facts, details, or claims which were unknown or unsuspected at the time this agreement was signed, and had I known at that time may have affected my decision to sign this agreement. I acknowledge and accept that by reason of this agreement, I am assuming any risk of such unknown facts, details, and claims unknown and unsuspected. Once I grant the rights outlined in this agreement, I understand and agree that my decision is irrevocable.

This agreement shall be interpreted under the internal, substantive law of the state of *Company's home state* without regard to the conflicts of law provisions thereof. The parties submit to the exclusive jurisdiction and venue of the state and federal courts located in *Company's home County, State*, and waive any objections that they may have as to jurisdiction or venue in any such courts.

This is the complete and binding agreement between Company and me and my child/ward, and it supersedes all prior understandings and communications, both oral and written, with respect to its subject matter. If any provisions of this agreement are found unenforceable this will not affect the validity or

80

enforceability of any of the remainder of this agreement, which shall be enforced to the maximum extent permitted by law. This agreement cannot be terminated, rescinded or amended, except by a written agreement signed by both Company and me.

I am of lawful age and have read and understand this Minor Appearance Authorization, Assignment, and Release.

81

Signature: _________________________________ Date: ___________

Print (Neatly): ____

Full Address: ____

Phone: ____

Location Release

As the owner, and/or authorized representative or tenant of the owner of the property ("Owner") located at _______________________________________
a.k.a. _______________ (name of premises/establishment), I grant unconditional permission to *COMPANY* ("Company") forever, to enter and use said premises/establishment ("Location") for shooting videos, photos, and capturing audio . Company has the sole right to grant third parties, subsidiaries and other associates up to and including the same rights and permissions granted to Company by this entire agreement. Once I grant the rights outlined in this agreement, I understand and agree that my decision is irrevocable.

Company promises to prevent damage to Location within reason and will reimburse Owner if damage does occur. Company agrees that Owner will not be held responsible or accountable for any claims of personal injuries or property damage as a result of negligence or willful misconduct of Company while Company is engaged in said use of the Location.

Objects at the Location such as furniture, signage, or the like may or may not need to be removed or changed at Company's sole discretion. Anything removed or changed by Company will be replaced by Company. Company can, but is not obligated to, include any branding signage, trade names, trademarks, copyrights and logos of Owner, or otherwise visible on Location in the photos, videos, and audio recordings ("material").

I understand and agree Company owns sole and complete rights and copyright ownership of the material shot on Location. I release any claim or rights to the material. I know Company doesn't have to use any of the material, but has sole discretion, without hinderance from anyone, to use the material without limits, for promotional, and audio/visual purposes, and can choose how and when to display the material in any way at any time in the future throughout the universe, and that's fine by me. The Company can also include my name if they want, in association with these materials too. If not, I'm cool. It's not an issue. The Company can use the material repeatedly and perpetually.

Neither Owner nor any tenant or any other party having an interest in the Location shall have any claim or action against Company or any other party due to use of the material acquired and used from said Location.

Owner represents and warrants that owner has the right to enter into this agreement and to grant Company all rights provided by this agreement. In the event that Owner is not the legal owner ("Master") of Location, Owner represents and warrants that Owner has secured from the Master the right and authority to enter into this agreement and to grant Company all rights provided hereunder. In the event that Owner has not in truth obtained the right and authority to enter into this agreement, Owner understands and agrees that Company will not be held responsible or accountable for any claims or demands from Master of Location, or any other party having an interest in Location for any reason whatsoever, and will defend Company legally and agree to pay any legal fees associated with the discovering of this untruthful act.

No other authorization is necessary to enable Company to use the Premises for the purpose aforementioned. Nothing in this agreement shall limit or restrict any rights otherwise enjoyed by Company under law or agreement.

This agreement shall be interpreted under the internal, substantive law of the state of *Company's home state* without regard to the conflicts of law provisions thereof. The parties submit to the exclusive jurisdiction and venue of the state and federal courts located in *Company's home County, State*, and waive any objections that they may have as to jurisdiction or venue in any such courts.

This is the complete and binding agreement between Company and Owner, and it supersedes all prior understandings and communications, both oral and written, with respect to its subject matter. If any provisions of this agreement are found unenforceable this will not affect the validity or enforceability of any of the remainder of this agreement, which shall be enforced to the maximum extent permitted by law. This agreement cannot be terminated, rescinded or amended, except by a written agreement signed by both Company and Owner.

I am of lawful age and have read and understand this Location Authorization, Assignment, and Release.

Signature: ______________________________ Date: ______________

Print (Neatly): ____

Full Address:____

Phone: ____

Existing Materials Release

I grant unconditional permission to *COMPANY* ("Company") forever, to reproduce, publicly distribute, publicly display, publicly perform, and create derivative works from my property or properties listed below:

("Licensed Material")

Company has the sole right to grant third parties, subsidiaries and other associates up to and including the same rights and permissions granted to Company by this entire agreement. Once I grant the rights outlined in this agreement, I understand and agree that my decision is irrevocable.

I willingly grant Company non-exclusive rights to use my Licensed Material whether in whole or in part, without limits. I know Company doesn't have to use any of my Licensed Material, but at it's sole discretion may choose to use the Licensed Material however it wishes for things like but not limited to promotional, and audio/visual purposes. Company can choose how and when to display the material in any way at any time in the future throughout the universe, and that's fine by me. The Company can also include my name if they want, in association with these materials too. If not, I'm cool. It's not an issue. The Company can use the material repeatedly and perpetually. I understand and agree that I'm granting these rights to Company on a royalty-free basis, and waive all claims or demands for any and all forms of compensation arising from my Licensed Material.

I am the sole owner, or authorized representative of the sole owner of the rights being granted in this agreement, including, but not limited to any and all copyrights, trademarks, and rights in the likenesses of any people (if any) depicted in the Licensed Material.

I am authorized to enter into and execute this agreement, that nothing of value apart from the Licensed Material was given (or was agreed to be given) to Company or any other person or entity in exchange for use of the Licensed Material, that the consent of no other person or entity is required to enable company to use the Licensed Material as described herein, and that such use will not violate the rights of any third parties.

I agree to hold Company harmless, legally defend Company if necessary, and pay all legal fees for Company due to any and all claims of any kind arising from the use of my Licensed Material including but not limited to, any and all claims of damages for libel, slander, and invasion of the right of privacy.

In the event that I am found not to be truthful to any and all statements in this agreement, I understand and agree that Company will not be held responsible or accountable for any and all claims or demands any other party having an interest in the Licensed Material for any reason whatsoever, and will legally defend Company and agree to pay any and all legal fees associated with the discovering of this untruthful act, until all litigation and payments have come to their completion.

No other authorization is necessary to enable Company to use the Licensed Material for the purpose aforementioned. Nothing in this agreement shall limit or restrict any rights otherwise enjoyed by Company under law or agreement.

This agreement shall be interpreted under the internal, substantive law of the state of *Company's home state* without regard to the conflicts of law provisions thereof. The parties submit to the exclusive jurisdiction and venue of the state and federal courts located in *Company's home County, State*, and waive any objections that they may have as to jurisdiction or venue in any such courts.

This is the complete and binding agreement between Company and myself, and it supersedes all prior understandings and communications, both oral and written, with respect to its subject matter. If any provisions of this agreement are found unenforceable this will not affect the validity or enforceability of any of the remainder of this agreement, which shall be enforced to the maximum extent permitted by law. This agreement cannot be terminated, rescinded or amended, except by a written agreement signed by both Company and Owner.

I am of lawful age and have read and understand this authorization and release.

Signature: _________________________________ Date: _______________

Print (Neatly): ____

Full Address: ____

Phone: ____

Posted Notice

Videography, Photography, and Audio Recording In Progress...

COMPANY is on location shooting photographs and videos, and recording audio of this event. This material may be used for promotional purposes in the future. You may, and most likely will, be included in multiple pictures and videos, and audio recordings. If you enter this event/space/location, you irrevocably grant *COMPANY* unconditional permission, without limits, to use your image and voice, and that of your children or wards image and voice if they are attending this event with you repeatedly and perpetually forever. *COMPANY* shall have sole discretion when, how, and where throughout the universe it wants to display these photographs, videos, and audio recordings.

THANK YOU!

- COMPANY

"Good Sound Keeping" Checklist:

"GOOD SOUND KEEPING" CHECKLIST:

No matter what you're using to record your audio, there is no excuse for not taking time to ensure that you're capturing the best sound possible. Below are some solutions that cost you **ABSOLUTELY NOTHING** to help you start making better audio recordings in your home today! And pretty much all of these tips work for capturing audio for video too!

Anything with quality takes time to prepare, and so the same goes for recording great audio…It all starts with how you set it up at the beginning because in the end, "it's hard to polish a turd" as the saying goes. So set yourself up for success!

Take Control Of Your environment:

Turn off any nearby appliances such as refrigerators, ceiling fans, etc. ESPECIALLY the furnace, or air conditioning.

Isolate you and your microphone as much as possible

Close Windows

Close the door to your room you are recording in if you can

Remember to:

Silence your cell phone…don't just put it on vibrate, but totally **silence** it.

Put your phone in airplane mode to avoid getting notifications that will divert your attention.

Really the best option would be to just turn it off — unless you absolutely need it for something.

If you have pets or small children, put them on "silent" as well…Benadryl anyone? Just kidding…but seriously…

Let others in your home know when you're recording. That way, you're less likely to have toilets flushing and herds of buffalo in the background. You HEAVY WALKERS know what I'm talking about! Put a sign on your doorbell even!

How many of us know our homes pretty well? We know the noises our home makes — any creaking, or settling noises that happen. If you can hear that with your ears, just know that **your microphone is like an ear on steroids.**

Hard surfaces are reflective surfaces — cover them as much as possible!
Tile or hardwood floors
Bare walls
Use thick blankets to cover what you can to "deaden" the room. MOVING BLANKETS ARE BEST!

If you don't treat the room, your microphone will "hear" the sound of your room, which means your recording might be loud, but it wouldn't be crisp — like your dry-cleaned fine linens…

Don't Be Your Own Worst Enemy:

Pay attention to your attire! *(Mainly for audio-only projects)*
Don't:
Wear starched shirts or slacks (You may like the crinkly but your recording won't), ticking watches, or jangly jewelry.

Take any loose change or keys out of your pockets

DO:
Wear a "silent" wardrobe. How many of you would like to wear your sweat pants to work? Or better yet, your PJs? When recording an audio-only project, you can! (Think cotton, like sweat pants and a comfy t-shirt.)

Remember to be still. You don't have to be a mannequin, but keep unnecessary shifting to a minimum.

Less moving = less undesirable noises.

It also helps keep your sound consistent. (Your proximity to the mic won't change much being still)

If you gesture a lot, that's ok. That will help add life to your message. Just be sure to keep in mind the earlier point about your clothing, and to gesture away from the mic.

Once all your equipment is in place, try not to change anything in that room until your entire project is done, as this can alter your sound.

If you have to move it, find a way to mark your room so you set everything up exactly the way it was when you continue your project. (This would include taking note of any settings on your gear as well.)

Don't smack! No one wants to hear you finishing up on the last meal you ate that day.

Other nasty mouth noises can occur naturally while you speak. If you're an offender, it's usually a sign of a dry mouth.

Have water nearby and drink it often to minimize these little distractions.

If they persist, try eating an apple. Apples can help minimize this. I hear green ones especially do the trick!

ESPECIALLY FOR AUDIO-ONLY PROJECTS: If you mess up on a line, just pause for a few seconds and start that line again.

ESPECIALLY FOR AUDIO-ONLY PROJECTS: If you're working from a script, reading your material from a tablet or smartphone helps to cut down on additional noise such as flipping pages using physical paper.

ESPECIALLY FOR AUDIO-ONLY PROJECTS: If working from a script, it's very easy to just read the words in front of you. Make your content "live"!
Breath life into your words, by:
Using pitch, pace, and power.
Emphasize key thoughts and words.
Speak the words to your listeners as if you are having a conversation with them, one on one — face to face.
Recording an audio-only projects is a "performance".
Since there are no visuals to accompany the material you have to keep it lively.

If you're material is pleasant in nature, try to keep a smile on your face while reading the script. Even though your listeners may not see it, they will definitely "hear" it coming through their headphones and speakers.

Speaking of making something live — standing is better than sitting. It creates more energy in your delivery. You'll be more expressive and inclined to use gestures and body language.

And finally, even after all of these precautions, there will still be distractions around you that you cannot control. The occasional police siren, neighbor firing up the lawnmower, just as you were finishing your perfect take! It happens, let them finish and try to record later when it's quiet, or if you know your neighbor well enough, you know what to do.

Non-Disclosure Agreements:

So this section in the index was really something I threw in last minute. As I was sharing the early drafts of my book with a few speakers that I work closely with on a regular basis, I wanted to make sure that my intellectual property would remain just that — my intellectual property. No matter how well acquainted you are with someone, you should always keep business, business, and everything above board. I drafted up a non-disclosure agreement and had them all sign it before sharing the manuscripts with them…and then I thought, this was something useful for all you speakers out there too!

As you come up with new products, other marketing ideas, and the like, you'll find that you may need to get other people or services involved. Obviously you don't want them running off with your valuable ideas and calling them their own hence the reason for an NDA. I would always suggest going to a licensed legal professional for assistance with this, but I've included the exact NDA I used when sharing this book before it was released, to give you a sample of the things to keep in mind when writing yours up! Check out the next page.

Non-Disclosure Agreement

I agree that any information disclosed to me by Clef Tone Grooves in connection with its book, which currently has a working title of *"Professional Audio Visual"* will be considered proprietary and confidential, including all such information relating to the Company's past, present, or future business activities, research, product design or development, personnel, marketing, and business opportunities.

Confidential information shall not include information previously known to me, the general public, or previously recognized as standard practice in the field.

I agree that until the book is made available for sale to the public, I will hold all confidential and proprietary information in confidence and will not use such information except as may be authorized by the Company and will prevent its unauthorized dissemination. I acknowledge that unauthorized disclosure could cause irreparable harm and significant injury to Clef Tone Grooves. I agree that upon request, I will destroy all written or descriptive matter, related to *"Professional Audio Visual"* and any supporting documents.

Accepted and agreed to by:

Signature: ____

Printed Name: _____________________________________

Title: ____

Company: ____

Date _______________

The Original Tone Setter

Darrin Thompson is the owner/ operator of Clef Tone Grooves (*www.ClefToneGrooves.com*). He started his company in June 2016 initially licensing his music from his website to artists. Over time, he started licensing his music to more and more life coaches and speakers as he's gotten to meet and work with them.

Darrin got his start in audio nearly 20 years ago when he realized he had too many instruments to play and not enough hands. He would riff on his sax, his bass, and his keyboard — coming up with lines on each of them that he knew, if he could just hear them all together, they would compliment each other beautifully. Eventually, he would add guitar to that mix. With no one else around to play those other instruments with him, he got to work learning how to record audio on his computer so he could lay the riffs down, track by track. Those tracks turned into songs, and the rest is history!

Over the years, he has grown his audio knowledge and skill level through mentors and self-directed learning to routinely produce professional grade audio recordings. Most recently in 2017 Darrin got the opportunity to be an audio engineer in the media department of a fortune 50 company.

10 years prior to this opportunity, Darrin landed a job as a production assistant in that same department where he's soaked up a ton of video production experience learning skills like set design, lighting, grip work, camera work, and many other aspects of Audio/Visual production — from gear to techniques! This is why he's able to speak to so much more than just audio, even though that's where his passion and main skillset lies.

Outside of the daily grind, and writing this book, Darrin has also released an EP of original music with his "partner in rhyme", Justin Grant, under the artist name of D&J. He's also released an album of his older music under that same artist name. He's done all of the mixing and mastering, and played most of the instruments on each track. The most popular songs by far from these projects are *Mexicali Queen,* and *Set Me Free.*

Darrin has also built a video series on youtube and Facebook called *"Get Better Audio At Home"* specifically aimed at helping coaches and speakers learn the skills, and gear necessary to improve their audio visual production quality.

NOTES

NOTES

NOTES

NOTES

NOTES

NOTES

SQUASH THE LEARNING CURVE, SPEED UP YOUR BREAKTHROUGH!

It's one thing to *read* about the techniques I discuss in my book, it's another to *hear* about them in the audiobook, and still yet another to *SEE THEM IN ACTION!*

That's why I've also created a video guide!!

I bring all the techniques I discuss in this book to life, showing you exactly how *TAKE YOUR AUDIO/VISUAL GAME TO A PROFESSIONAL LEVEL!*

You will learn:

- How to professionally capture audio for video
- Which microphone(s) you should buy for video and how to get the most out of them
- Lighting yourself and your set
- Basic anti-shine makeup for TV/Film

You also get TWO COMPLIMENTARY BONUSES!
- An in-depth introduction/tutorial to shooting your videos with a DSLR Camera (*If you shoot all of your videos with a webcam or cell phone like EVERYONE ELSE these days, then YOU'VE GOTTA SEE THIS!*)
- My Basic Audio Kit Overview

Learn:

- What kind of microphone(s) and other gear to buy for Audio-only projects
- A step-by-step guide to installing the gear I recommend
- How you can RECORD YOUR NEXT AUDIOBOOK WITH ME IN STUDIO QUALITY ONLINE!